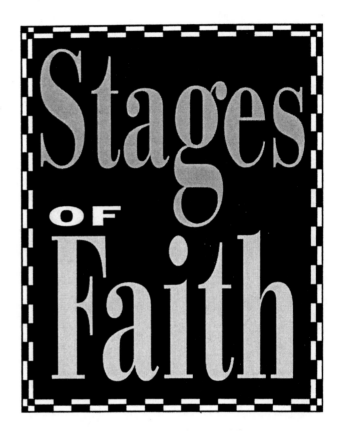

Eight Milestones Mark Your Journey

A Powerful Resource for Small-Group or Personal Use

By Don Willett, Ph.D.

To order copies of *Stages of Faith*, the Spiritual Growth Profile, write or call:

Don Willett, Ph.D.
408 North Broadway, Suite E
Redondo Beach, CA 90277
(310) 374-5953

e-mail: don.willett@roadrunner.com

Check out the website at:
www.stagesoffaith.com

Other available resources include, for group leaders, a Leader's Guide, for teachers, a CD of Power Point slides to supplement each lesson, and, for anyone interested, "The Case for Stages," a biblical defense of the apostle John's three stages of spiritual growth.

Acknowledgements
I would like to thank Mel Andrews for his design of the *Stages of Faith* logo;
John Hamilton for his input on graphics, layout, and design; and Lisa Guest for her editorial work. These three talented people have contributed much to this project.

Table of Contents

Preface

If you've been a Christian for any length of time, you're probably familiar with discipleship materials of various kinds—and you may even be disillusioned and discouraged—because of some of them.

◆ Have you jumped through prescribed spiritual hoops—more commitment, more surrender, more Bible study, more prayer, more giving, more doing, more attendance, more witness, more memorization—and still found your faith not as fulfilling and freeing as you sense it could be?

◆ You may be tired of simplistic, fill-in-the-blank exercises and leading questions which prompt the "right" answers.

◆ Maybe you've noticed that materials fail to describe or address how the journey of faith progresses over a lifetime, especially adulthood, the longest period of life.

◆ Maybe you're disenchanted with discipleship materials that do not address our inner need for wholeness and for healing from old hurts.

Well, keep reading! *Stages of Faith* is different!

First of all, *Stages of Faith* offers a compelling agenda of basics for Christian growth and a fresh map for you to follow on the journey. Based on 1 John 2:12-14, *Stages of Faith* outlines three stages of spiritual growth and the milestones that define each stage. As author John Stott has noted about these three verses, the apostle John identified "stages in their spiritual development... three different stages of spiritual pilgrimage." [1]

Adulthood offers us a unique opportunity to experience in ever-deepening ways the profound truths of our Christian faith, and a genuine spirituality that is genuinely transformative. After all, we shouldn't expect our experience of faith in our younger years to suffice in our later years—and that's not God's plan either.

Stages of Faith is designed to stimulate personal spiritual growth. Its content and questions are intended to help you think about your faith at higher levels and live out in your attitudes and behaviors the biblical lessons you learn.

You will find the material challenging, and you will work hard along the way as you think in new and different ways about your faith. But you won't be in it alone! This workbook is a tool, you may have a partner or small group traveling with you, and all of us have available to us the power of prayer and the company of the Holy Spirit, our Teacher and Counselor. So don't give up! God wants you to grow in your faith, to grow in your relationship with Him, and this guide can help you experience such growth and receive the blessings that come with it.

Who will benefit from *Stages of Faith*?

Pastors, small-group leaders, Christian counselors, Christian educators, parents, children's and youth workers, and teachers—all of whom are faith-shapers—will benefit from the biblical model of spiritual growth outlined here.

Stages of Faith also offers you, the individual, a map for your spiritual journey, but is designed for a group of people who want to travel this journey of growth together. But what exactly is the goal of spiritual maturity—and what can we do to help our fellow Christians get there? And how can we determine where we ourselves are on the journey toward Christlikeness and spiritual maturity? We need biblical benchmarks by which we can identify our spiritual strengths as well as any unfinished business that may be slowing our growth. Each lesson here includes questions that can prompt lively discussion. As group members get to know one another at a new level, they can support and challenge each other along the way. (The "Tips for the Small-Group Leader" section, pages 115-119), is included to help the group experience be more worthwhile.)

Furthermore, pastors and church leaders will find in *Stages of Faith* a biblical model by which to appraise the health and growth of their congregation. *Stages of Faith* can also help them determine what they are doing to produce spiritually mature Christians, whether their programs are fostering spiritual growth, what is delaying growth in their people, and what they can do to enrich their ministry and encourage movement toward spiritual maturity.

The Spiritual Growth Profile

Key to getting the most out of Stages of Faith is the Spiritual Growth Profile, a unique instrument for measuring one's progress in each of the three stages. No other tool like this profile exists! When you complete the profile and evaluate the results—and you'll do so before you begin Lesson 1—you will see more clearly where you are in the Childhood, Young Adulthood and Parenthood stages of faith. This workbook will then help you plan for ongoing growth.

My doctoral degree in Educational Studies (a Ph.D. from Talbot School of Theology); my seventeen years of teaching *Stages of Faith* in churches, seminaries and Christian universities; and feedback from many small groups have brought *Stages of Faith* to this point. Where I currently pastor, I am responsible for discipleship and spiritual formation with an emphasis on *Stages of Faith*.

Again, you'll be working hard at different points of *Stages of Faith*, but don't give up! After all, anything worth doing is going to demand some effort—and this is definitely worth doing! Your journey of faith may never be the same again!

Please keep in touch with me as you journey toward Christlikeness and a greater ability to provide spiritual guidance to others.

Don Willett, Ph.D.
December, 2007

Lesson 1

Stages of Faith: An Overview
A Model of Spiritual Growth

Whenever we go someplace we've never been, we need a map to get there. That fact is just as true in the spiritual realm as it is in the physical world. But how many of us are relying on a map for our spiritual journey? Do you know where you're going in your spiritual life? If so, what are you doing to get there? What roads are you traveling so that you're sure you arrive at your chosen destination?

You hope that you're growing to know God better and that you're becoming more like Christ. You may even be disciplined about Bible study, prayer, witnessing, and fellowship to ensure that you're growing in your faith—and that's wonderful. But, with the help of John the apostle, I would like to offer you a new perspective, a biblical map by which you and I can chart our course for the lifelong journey of spiritual growth.

In his first epistle to early believers, the apostle John offered Christians then—and offers us today—a map of spiritual growth. He outlined God's agenda for a believer's transformational journey. This journey happens in three stages: Childhood, Young Adulthood, and Parenthood. John identified various milestones for each of these stages, and these milestones serve as benchmarks on the road to spiritual maturity.

As you work through these thirteen lessons, you will come to:

- ◆ Understand a biblical map of the lifelong journey of spiritual growth
- ◆ Pinpoint how far you have come in each of the three stages
- ◆ Identify the obstacles that are delaying your spiritual progress in each stage and plan some ways to overcome these obstacles as you travel on your journey
- ◆ Discover how you can skillfully guide others toward maturity and Christlikeness
- ◆ Learn how to continue to grow in your faith during your adult years

The First Step!

Grab a pencil and your Spiritual Growth Profile and complete the form. Instructions for tabulating and interpreting the results are provided. I'll encourage you to look back at your profile whenever I introduce a new milestone, so I'm confident that you'll soon see what a valuable tool it is. It will probably take you forty minutes to complete the profile—and know that it's time well invested.

Aims of Lesson #1

Plan to spend about two hours completing this lesson and preparing for your small-group time. During your time of personal study, you will:

◆ Come to better understand the idea of having a map for your spiritual journey

◆ Think through the foundational ideas found in 1 John and consider their relevance to your own spiritual growth and

◆ Familiarize yourself with the eight milestones of the Christian journey outlined by the apostle John

For Small-Group Leaders:

We recommend that during the ninety-minute study portion of this meeting, group members discuss the following questions.

Lesson 1
1-8

You will not be able to give equal time to each question. So, as the group leader, budget your time carefully.

The Journey According to John

Our journey of faith begins at salvation and does not end until our physical death and heavenly glorification, when we become fully like Christ (1 John 3:2). Until then we believers are in various stages of spiritual growth or Christlikeness.

In 1 John 2:12-14, the seasoned apostle John offers us a map of the journey of faith. This map can help us chart our progress through the three stages of spiritual development. All believers are either in the Childhood, Young Adulthood, or Parenthood stage of faith. Some of us are more like Christ, more mature and farther along than others, but all of us have room to grow.

What follows is a description of five key aspects of authentic spirituality found in the passage from 1 John. Let God, through John's words, challenge your present understanding of the Christian life, what it means to be "spiritual," and how to grow in your faith.

1 Friendship in Two Directions– 1 John 1:1-4

1 What was from the beginning, what we have heard, what we have seen with our eyes, what we have looked at and touched with our hands, concerning the Word of Life— 2 and the life was manifested, and we have seen and testify and proclaim to you the eternal life, which was with the Father and was manifested to us— 3 what we have seen and heard we proclaim to you also, so that you too may have fellowship with us; and indeed our fellowship is with the Father, and with His Son Jesus Christ. 4 These things we write, so that our joy may be made complete.

The purpose of the Incarnation—of Jesus coming to earth in human form—was to fully reveal God to us. The apostles—whose words we read in the New Testament—saw, heard, and touched Jesus and therefore offer conclusive and compelling evidence that He was fully and genuinely both God and man. As they interacted with Jesus, they invited people (and that includes us today) to develop friendships in two directions—friendship with God and friendship with fellow believers. We are to know and love Jesus *and* know and love one another. We find real joy (1:4) in the combined experiences of our vertical relationship with God and our horizontal relationship with brothers and sisters in Christ. "Jesus and Me" is a very personal and intimate relationship, but it should never be exclusively private. "Jesus and We" is richly interpersonal and communal.

 Why are both friendship with God (Jesus and Me) and friendship with His people (Jesus and We) important to spiritual growth? What if one is either neglected or overemphasized?

2 Living Without Pretense – 1 John 1:5-2:2

5 This is the message we have heard from Him and announce to you, that God is Light, and in Him there is no darkness at all. 6 If we say that we have fellowship with Him and yet walk in the darkness, we lie and do not practice the truth; 7 but if we walk in the Light as He Himself is in the Light, we have fellowship with one another, and the blood of Jesus His Son cleanses us from all sin. 8 If we say that we have no sin, we are deceiving ourselves and the truth is not in us. 9 If we confess our sins, He is faithful and righteous to forgive us our sins and to cleanse us from all unrighteousness. 10 If we say that we have not sinned, we make Him a liar and His word is not in us. 2:1 My little children, I am writing these things to you so that you may not sin. And if anyone sins, we have an Advocate with the Father, Jesus Christ the righteous; 2 and He Himself is the propitiation for our sins; and not for ours only, but also for those of the whole world.

In sharp contrast to our dark and twisted human nature, God is described as pure and flawless light (1 John 1:5). The God who invites us into an intimate relationship with Him is absolutely holy and morally perfect. His light exposes our darkness. Since we are fully known by Him, there is no use in trying to hide from Him—yet we often try to do just that. But we can—and must—be open about who we are, about our sin and our love of darkness, if we are to know Jesus deeply. Authentic spirituality invites us to a bold integrity, truthfulness, transparency, and vulnerability.

But this aspect of genuine spirituality—bold integrity, truthfulness, transparency, and vulnerability with a holy God—can sound a little threatening. What are our options?

Downward Spiral: One option is to ignore, deny, excuse, or defend our sinfulness and the deep needs which both underlie and accompany that sinfulness (1 John 1:6,8,10). We are often too insecure and cowardly to admit that we are powerless over our hurts, our habits, and our hungerings. But John warned that pretense gradually leads us away from truth and repair and toward deeper illusion, deceit, and darkness. It is costly to fail to honestly admit to ourselves, to God, and to others our sins, our inconsistencies, and our rationalizations of these failings. Slow to drop our masks and pretense, we fail to walk in God's way. We live on a downward spiral.

Upward Spiral: When we see the enormity of our sinfulness and our dismal failure to be like Jesus, our other option is to candidly and courageously admit those failings to God (1 John 1:7,9; 2:1). When we do so, God forgives us, cleanses us, and reshapes us more into His likeness. Having confessed our sin (which is something we need to do daily!) and professed to know Jesus as our Savior and Lord, we must then support with our actions our claim to know Him personally. In other words, our pursuit of holiness is not optional. We are to learn to walk according to God's ways and in His light.

As we do so, we progressively experience a grace-based Christian life. We discard our masks and become real. Clearly, the basis of our relationship with God is not our sinlessness, but His unexpected, undeserved and ongoing forgiveness of our sin. Growing Christians learn to make this unconditional love— this grace—the basis of their day-to-day experience. Fully forgiven and accepted by our holy God, we can enjoy an intimate relationship with Him. We need not be threatened and intimidated by His holiness. We can face both the bad news about our sin and the pain of our woundedness as we keep before us the good news of God's total acceptance of us through Christ. We can live without pretense.

 Why is learning to live without pretense important to spiritual growth?

#3 Evidence of Genuine Faith – 1 John 2:3-11, 18-27

3 By this we know that we have come to know Him, if we keep His commandments. 4 The one who says, "I have come to know Him," and does not keep His commandments, is a liar, and the truth is not in him; 5 but whoever keeps His word, in him the love of God has truly been perfected. By this we know that we are in Him: 6 the one who says he abides in Him ought himself to walk in the same manner as He walked. 7 Beloved, I am not writing a new commandment to you, but an old commandment which you have had from the beginning; the old commandment is the word which you have heard. 8 On the other hand, I am writing a new commandment to you, which is true in Him and in you, because the darkness is passing away and the true Light is already shining. 9 The one who says he is in the Light and yet hates his brother is in the darkness until now. 10 The one who loves his brother abides in the Light and there is no cause for stumbling in him. 11 But the one who hates his brother is in the darkness and walks in the darkness, and does not know where he is going because the darkness has blinded his eyes.

In these verses, John identified two of three kinds of evidence that a person truly knows God, three indications of authentic spirituality. (The third is mentioned in verses 18-27.) Three times in his brief letter John elaborated on these three types of evidence. We cannot afford to miss the apostle's emphasis: These truths are to increasingly shape our lives. Too, each of these three "tests" show us that we have lots of room for growth.

• Obedience—**walking as Jesus walked**—is evidence of genuine faith. Those of us who claim to have a friendship with God increasingly prove it by our actions, not just by an orthodox profession (2:3-6; 2:28-3:10; 5:2-3). Looking honestly at how obedient we're being helps us evaluate our spiritual progress in the vertical dimension of our faith—Jesus and Me. We are to become more and more like Him in our conduct. As we let go of pretense, we can honestly admit where our ways do not resemble His.

• Love—**loving as Jesus loved**—is further evidence that we truly know Him. Those of us who claim to be His children will progressively demonstrate that we are His children by our love for other people (2: 7-11; 3:11-18; 4:7-5:3). Looking honestly at how loving we are helps us evaluate our spiritual progress in the horizontal dimension of faith—Jesus and We. We are to increasingly resemble Him in caring for others. As we let go of pretense, we can admit—and confess and be forgiven of—our self-absorption and self-centeredness.

• Discernment is **seeing as Jesus sees**, and that is the third kind of evidence that we are in relationship with Him. Those of us who claim to follow God will progressively demonstrate the reality of that claim by discerning counterfeits to faith, identifying lies about God's truth, and noting false teaching about Christ's character and mission (2:18-27; 4:1-6; 5:1,4,5). There will also be a movement away from reliance on teachers in order to gain a firsthand, carefully examined faith (2:27). We will increasingly see all of life as Jesus does.

 What does 1 John 2:3-11 help you better understand about spiritual growth? What have these verses helped you notice about your own growth?

#4 Progress Through Three Stages of Spiritual Growth – 1 John 2:12-14

12 I am writing to you, little children, because your sins have been forgiven you for His name's sake. 13 I am writing to you, fathers, because you know Him who has been from the beginning. I am writing to you, young men, because you have overcome the evil one. I have written to you, children, because you know the Father. 14 I have written to you, fathers, because you know Him who has been from the beginning. I have written to you, young men, because you are strong, and the word of God abides in you, and you have overcome the evil one.

Walking in total obedience to God just as Jesus walked, loving as He loves, seeing as He sees—we all fall short of these three standards so often! In fact, they seem completely unattainable. No wonder John was quick to reassure his readers of their salvation! He reiterated that we are in the family of God and that we can rest assured of that fact.

John also addressed the fact that some of God's family are farther along in their faith journey and spiritual growth than others of us are. The apostle describes three discrete stages of spiritual growth. Some Christians are in the Childhood stage, some are in the Young Adulthood stage, and others are in the Parenthood stage in their spiritual progress. John Stott observes that the apostle John "is indicating not their physical

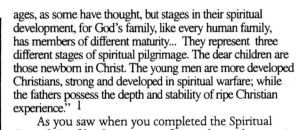

ages, as some have thought, but stages in their spiritual development, for God's family, like every human family, has members of different maturity... They represent three different stages of spiritual pilgrimage. The dear children are those newborn in Christ. The young men are more developed Christians, strong and developed in spiritual warfare; while the fathers possess the depth and stability of ripe Christian experience." [1]

As you saw when you completed the Spiritual Growth Profile, these stages of growth are characterized by specific milestones (also see the chart on page 7), and completion of the tasks identified at each of these eight milestones contributes to our growth in holiness and wholeness. These milestones will be the focus of this thirteen-lesson study.

Why can understanding the three stages of spiritual growth help that growth happen?

#5 The Enemies of Spiritual Growth – 1 John 2:15-17

15 Do not love the world nor the things in the world. If anyone loves the world, the love of the Father is not in him. 16 For all that is in the world, the lust of the flesh and the lust of the eyes and the boastful pride of life, is not from the Father, but is from the world. 17 The world is passing away, and also its lusts; but the one who does the will of God lives forever.

The journey of faith takes place on a very real battleground. As 1 John 2:15-17 warns, whether we are in the Childhood, Young Adulthood, or Parenthood stage of faith, we can be sure to encounter three rivals to our growth—the world, the flesh, and the devil. This trinity of evil can indeed be hazardous to your spiritual progress. Furthermore, in verses 18-27, John warned about the false teachers who deceive and about false believers who defect from the faith. No wonder he called us Christians to develop discernment (2:18-27; 4:1-6; 5:1,4,5).

Finally, we need to remember that spiritual growth is never automatic and that we are never too mature to be seduced by these persistent and pervasive enemies. Our progress toward deeper and more genuine faith can definitely be impaired by the world, the flesh, and the devil, Awareness of this reality is the first step toward a healthy defense against those enemies.

 Why is the truth of 1 John 2:15-17 important to spiritual growth?

Summary: Five Aspects of Authentic Spirituality. In the verses we've been looking at, the apostle John touched on the following five traits of authentic Christianity:
• **Friendship**: vertically with God and horizontally with fellow believers;
• A life of vulnerability and **transparency** without pretense;
• **Evidence of genuine faith**: obedience, love, and perspective;
• **Progress** through three stages of spiritual growth;
• **Victory over the enemies** of spiritual growth: the world, the flesh, and the devil.

Every one of us who names Jesus as Savior and Lord is at a different point of growth in each of these categories, and each one of us has room to grow and progress. By God's grace, we have the power of His Spirit working within us to help that growth happen!

 Having read about these five aspects of authentic spirituality, which one do you find most interesting and/or most challenging? Explain your choice.

An Overview of Three Stages of Faith

Now some of you may be "chart people," and others of you may find charts overwhelming. Whichever category you find yourself, do take the time to read through the adjacent chart. Doing so will help the following points make a lot more sense. (Yes, this is one of those demanding parts of the book that I warned you about in the preface!)

The Parenthood

Stage: *Modeling Faith*

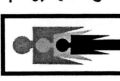

Milestone #7
Empowering Others

To grow spiritually, I need to assume my responsibility to impact other members of God's family, offering experience from my own spiritual journey and guided by the biblical principles of spiritual growth that are reflected in these milestones of faith. I will work to acquire the skills I need to effectively nurture my brothers and sisters toward Christlikeness and wholeness.

Milestone #8
Seasoned by Time and Experience

To grow spiritually, I need to press on, continuing to work on the milestone tasks of spiritual development so that I may know God better. I will not be content to let myself plateau and relax as the years go by. Instead, I will nurture a deepening relationship with my heavenly Father.

Stages of Spiritual Growth

The Young Adulthood

Stage: *The Ownership of Faith*

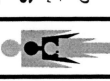

Milestone #4
Owning a Firsthand Faith

To grow spiritually, I need to establish ownership of a distinct, personal faith. Having worked through Milestones #1, #2, and #3, I now have a healthy foundation on which to continue to build my faith. My need to conform will diminish as I rely on biblical principles I have examined and internalized as my own.

Milestone #5
Linking Truth and Life

To grow spiritually, I need to allow God's Word to transform me. I will therefore move beyond merely receiving head knowledge from the Bible to, by the power of the Holy Spirit, applying its truth to my life. The Word of God will reside in me and have a centering and guiding influence on me.

Milestone #6
Defeating the Enemies of Spiritual Growth

To grow spiritually, I need to understand the lethal strategy of my three arch enemies—the world, the flesh, and the devil—and be willing to do battle against each of them. Knowing that healthy spiritual growth is impaired by neglecting or inadequately completing the milestones of spiritual development, I will continue to work on the core issues they address.

The Childhood

Stage: *The Birth of Faith*

Milestone #1
Experiencing God's Grace and Forgiveness

To grow spiritually, I need to believe that I am loved unconditionally. Once I am certain of God's forgiveness and confident that He accepts me in Christ, I will be able to discard pretense and my masks and receive His healing.

Milestone #2
Embracing God as Father

To grow spiritually, I need to know God as my Father, as the One in whom I can trust and to whom I can surrender my life. In order to know God as Father, I will replace my distorted ideas of God with biblical truth about Him and then let my heavenly Father re-parent me.

Milestone #3
Growing Up Together

To grow spiritually, I need to experience the mutually supportive and challenging relationships that can be found in the family of God. After all, we who are God's children grow whole when we're in community, not in isolation. We really do need one another.

7

As you saw, the chart's three columns list milestones of spiritual growth and which stage they fall into, Childhood, Young Adulthood, or Parenthood. These milestones, the focus of the next twelve lessons, are markers along the journey of faith. Together these milestones offer a compelling picture of the journey of faith, as this overview reveals.

Characteristics of Stages of Faith

The following ten premises will help you better understand this rich model of stages of spiritual growth, yet you will find no trace of simplistic formulas or canned prescriptions. The stages of spiritual growth:

Are common to all believers. Based on the teachings of God's Word, the stages reflect the experience of every Christian through the centuries and across various cultures. This is not a Western model or a trendy approach. First John 2:12-14 reflects the timeless truth that Christians are to continuously grow in faith throughout their lives.

Describe and explain both the content and the process of spiritual growth. What does normal, healthy spiritual growth look like and how does transformation occur? John's three stages contain vital clues to God's prescribed path for our lifelong journey of faith. The milestones offer benchmarks by which we can reliably assess our growth as well as chart our course for further progress. We will consider the possibilities and demands of each milestone that are basic to personal renewal — as well as the rhythms, patterns, contours, and seasons of the process of spiritual growth. Understanding and attending to each of the eight milestones can powerfully shape our lifelong development into the Christlike people God want us to be.

Are passed through by all of us in the same order. The Child stage precedes the Young Adult stage which, in turn, precedes the Parent stage, but this progression is no lockstep model of growth. Instead there is ongoing, concurrent interaction between the milestones, both within each stage as well as between the stages. This interaction is best thought of as a spiral rather than a straight line or even a staircase progression. Also, we aren't to expect an easy or seamless transition from one stage to the next, and we can't skip or rush through a stage or milestone without undermining our spiritual growth. Neither are there child prodigies or any spiritual elite on the journey of faith. All of us must attend to each milestone and every stage. Stated more strongly, there are no shortcuts to your growth in wholeness and Christlikeness.

Build on one another, each stage serving as a foundation for the next and each stage incorporating the preceding. Not only do the milestones fuel each other, but our failure to attend to them gives them the power to slow or even prevent our progress. Therefore, laying a strong foundation for faith during the Childhood stage is critical to our future growth. Also, we can expect to return to the dynamic milestones of the stages of Child, Young Adult, and Parent throughout our journey of faith. In God's refining process, we never seem to completely outgrow a stage. Thus, you are likely living in the midst of more than one stage simultaneously, though you will find yourself predominantlty in one stage.

Move us toward maturity, wholeness, and Christlikeness. The stages model is clear about the goal and the process. Along our journey toward authentic faith, we stop pretending, and we face and resolve as best we can the significant hurts, unhealthy habits, and unfulfilled hungerings in our lives, all of which block our growth. Also, as we progress through the stages of faith, we change. The Young Adult and the Parent, for instance, see and experience life more fully than the Child. Each stage brings a new capacity for growth. However, we need to be careful to value each stage for its unique richness and we need to remember that growth is not a race. The stages of faith do not comprise a ladder of achievement to climb as fast as we can. After all, we won't become fully mature and completely like Christ until our death or Christ's return (1 John 3:2-3).

Are linked to our age, but flexibly so. The "children," "young men," and "fathers" of 1 John 2:12-14 are metaphorical stages of spiritual growth, stages that have an age-linked component. But chronological age does provide clues to the stage of one's spiritual progress, and each new milestone emphasizes our readiness to deal with the spiritual task at hand. Consider these scenarios.

1.) Twelve-year-old Matt will not move beyond the Childhood stage of faith until he develops a greater sense of self, God, and others (the three milestones of the Childhood stage of faith).

2.) Chris, age twenty-five, is active in teaching and discipleship in the high-school youth group and plans to head into full-time ministry. Chris *may* have adequately attended to the milestones of the Childhood stage of faith, and he may be owning his faith in the Young Adulthood stage. But it isn't likely that Chris—or anyone else—will have the consistent and coherent faith of the Young Adult stage until after the mid-twenties or into the early thirties. We are likely to enter the stage of Parenthood after the age of forty if we've attended to the milestones of Childhood and Young Adulthood. So years of time and experience remain to fashion Chris into a seasoned Parent in the faith.

3.) Cindy just became a Christian at age fifty. She needs, then, to attend to the three milestones of the Childhood stage of faith in order to renew her concept of self, God, and others.

4.) Wendy has been a Christian for fifty years, but she may be stuck in the stage of Childhood, or she may have plateaued in Young Adulthood. Her chronological age does not guarantee that she is a Parent in the faith. Advancing in years does not automatically bring spiritual maturity.

Growth is *always* one of a kind. As I've said, each of us will pass through the same stages in the same order but not in the same way. There are substantial differences among believers as to when and how stages are experienced. Also, our personal tempos and the intensity of our growth will differ. After all, our spiritual growth is triggered by our unique life experiences, impactful events, and turning points which do not occur at any predictable or scheduled time. In seasons of challenge, if not pain, we are most susceptible to change. As we do change and let go of old ways, we may experience emotions ranging from apprehension, disenchantment, or fear to feelings of deliverance, relief, and excitement. Whatever the emotions, we may be realizing a deeper faith.

Growth is *not continuous*. John's stage model does not suggest a lockstep concept of growth, nor does it point to continuous, steady, seamless, and smooth transitions from one milestone or stage to the next. Growth may happen that way, but growth is at times irregular, and some change will occur more rapidly during certain periods and less rapidly during others. We can expect to experience seasons of stagnation, deterioration of old ways, and periods of fresh beginnings.

Growth is *not inevitable*. Spiritual growth is not automatic. Neither is it irreversible. The process of growth can be interrupted, crippled, stalled, and even reversed. In fact, neglecting or inadequately dealing with, any one of these milestones poses a real danger to spiritual growth. Unfinished business at one stage will make it difficult to resolve the next stage successfully. But we do not have to permanently plateau or stagnate. The apostle John set forth a map and invited us to travel toward God, but our journey is up to us.

Stages of growth *can be measured*. The Spiritual Growth Profile is a one-of-a-kind instrument that can help you both see your progress and health in the Childhood, Young Adulthood, and Parenthood stages of faith as well as identify any unfinished business that is slowing your growth. You will be encouraged where you are making progress and can plan to take steps to confidently go farther.

 Of the ten characteristics of stages of faith, which is of greatest interest or promises to be most helpful to you in understanding how spiritual growth happens? Explain.

The Metaphor of a Map

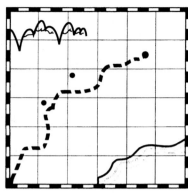

Just as a trail map guides our mountain hikes, the apostle John's biblical map can help guide our journey of faith. For instance, as we hike, we depend on a map to determine how far we've traveled. A map also helps us not get lost along the way. John's spiritual trail map does the same things for us as we journey and grow in our faith. A trail map, however, does not consider our age, how healthy we are, what kind of shape we're in, nor how experienced or motivated we are as we tackle the mountain hike. A map does not report weather conditions that may affect our journey, nor does it indicate how much time it may take to get to your destination. Likewise, John's spiritual map is not able to do any of these things in our journey. We who are hiking must therefore take note of these variables as we follow John's map and this *Stages of Faith* book.

Although you can work through this book in thirteen weeks, the journey of faith that it encourages will last a lifetime. And your journey will prove rich and rewarding as you set your sights on Jesus Christ—the goal of your faith—and call on the Holy Spirit to bless your travels.

 Now that you have been introduced to John's trail map, what is one goal you have for yourself? What is one thing you hope will result from working through these thirteen lessons? What do you hope God will do in your life as you journey through these lessons?

Lesson 2

Milestone #1 Experiencing Grace and Forgiveness
Part 1

The Childhood Stage:
The Birth of Faith

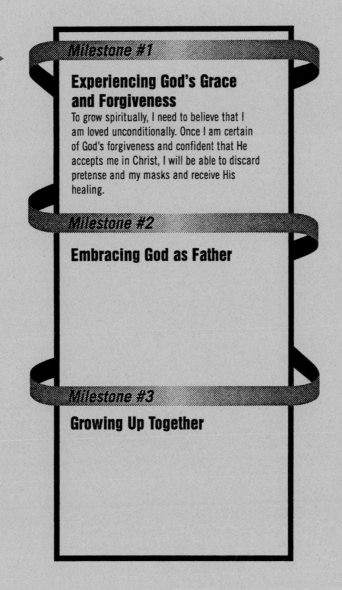

Milestone #1

Experiencing God's Grace and Forgiveness

To grow spiritually, I need to believe that I am loved unconditionally. Once I am certain of God's forgiveness and confident that He accepts me in Christ, I will be able to discard pretense and my masks and receive His healing.

Milestone #2

Embracing God as Father

Milestone #3

Growing Up Together

The first milestone of the Childhood stage of faith involves **renewing your self-concept** based on the truth of Scripture. This lesson helps you identify the warped mirrors that have shaped the way you see and consequently feel about yourself. You need to discard any inaccurate and distorted ideas about yourself that you learned from these lying mirrors and replace them with the image of yourself that you will only find in the truth-speaking mirror of God's Word.

Aims of Lesson #2

Plan to spend about two hours completing this lesson and preparing for your small-group time. During your time of personal study, you will:

♦ Learn about the first milestone in the Childhood stage of faith

♦ Establish or re-establish the biblical basis for your assurance of salvation and your status as a son/daughter of God

♦ Evaluate the extent of your personal experience of God's love and forgiveness

♦ Identify any warped mirrors that have distorted your identity and therefore jeopardize your spiritual as well as personal growth

♦ Look into the transforming mirror of God's truth in which you can begin to see yourself as He sees you

For Small-Group Leaders:

We recommend that during the ninety-minute study portion of this meeting, group members discuss the following questions.

Lesson 2
1-3, 5-8

You will not be able to give equal time to each question. So, as the group leader, budget your time carefully.

☑ Note:

Before reading through this Milestone, take a moment to glance at your **Spiritual Growth Profile**. Looking briefly at that mirror to your spiritual journey will help you put the coming discussion into the more personal context of your own spiritual growth.

The Childhood Stage of Spiritual Growth

Childhood is a time of intense learning. Think about all that you learned during those early years—everything from holding up your head and walking to learning to read, tie your shoes, and play baseball. You were exposed to many new ideas and skills, many of them fundamental to life.

Similarly, during the Childhood stage of our faith, we need to learn many lessons that are fundamental to a lifetime of spiritual growth. Often, however, we don't learn these lessons well. The three milestones of Childhood will help you learn or review key truths that serve as the foundation for your walk of faith. Working through these milestones and deeply personalizing the truths they teach is essential in the Childhood stage of faith.

Milestone #1 – Experiencing God's Grace and Forgiveness: A New Way of Relating to Self (two lessons)

Milestone #2 – Embracing God as Father: A New Way of Relating to God (one lesson)

Milestone #3 – Growing Up Together: A New Way of Relating to Others (two lessons)

Building a Guardrail for the Journey

The journey of faith takes us through various types of terrain. We'll encounter green valleys, lovely meadows, gentle hills, rocky paths, and steep mountains. When the going gets tough on those mountain passes of faith, it is important to have a guardrail alongside the path we're on. The three milestones of the Childhood stage of faith listed above form the guardrail we need so we can go farther and climb higher on our journey. Each of us Christians needs to be sure that these three milestones are securely in place if we are to progress to full mature faith.

The three milestones of Childhood give shape to the critical formative years of faith. The first two milestones contribute to the development of a distinctively Christian identity, the first one speaking to your perception and feelings about yourself and the second, to your perception and feelings about God. As these milestones define the vertical dimension of your faith, they also give internal structure to your life and motivation for your spiritual growth. Next, Milestone #3 encourages the development of distinctively Christian relationships, the horizontal dimension of faith. With its focus on intimacy, this milestone gives external structure to your life and motivation for living out your faith.

Why are these three milestones of the Childhood stage of faith important to our spiritual growth? First of all, these milestones comprise God's agenda for personal renewal. They also serve as the divine curriculum for spiritual birth and new life in Christ. Put differently, these three milestones are the foundation for the Young Adulthood and Parenthood stages—and therefore determine the quality of our future spiritual growth. Second, God uses these milestone tasks to heal us, free us, and move us toward wholeness and Christlikeness. We can expect our growth in the faith to be delayed if these three milestones tasks are neglected or unfinished. Many of us who are adults chronologically may have given inadequate attention to these milestone tasks and need to tend to some unfinished business in each.

Childhood Is Forever

Throughout our life, we will return again and again to each of the three milestones of Childhood for enrichment and reworking. Life events will trigger our need for renewal and for grounding ourselves once again in God's truth about who we are as His children.

We will never outgrow these basic truths, and any progress we make along our journey toward spiritual maturity depends on having this three-part guardrail in place.

Overview of Milestone #1
Experiencing God's Grace and Forgiveness: A New Way of Relating to Self

Based on 1 John 2:12 ("I am writing to you, little children, because your sins have been forgiven you for His name's sake"), Milestone #1 addresses the core issue of your self-concept, your identity. The truth to be learned here is "I am significant as God's son/daughter. I am unconditionally loved by Him I am absolutely secure in His love."

Moving Away From... Milestone #1 involves the process of moving away from dys-grace and toxic faith—from your sense that you are ineligible for God's love and forgiveness; from self-condemnation and self-justification; from being motivated by reward and punishment; from performing to please, and an addiction to approval; from the legalism and tyranny of "ought"; from pretense; and from shame-based living that sabotages our adult lives.

Moving Toward... At the same time that you move away from dys-grace and toxic faith in Milestone #1, you will move toward grace-based living—toward reprogramming your thinking about yourself based on God's grace and truth; toward finding security and significance as a son/daughter of God; toward confidence in God's certain, unconditional, and nonrepayable love; and toward experiencing divine healing of any crippling hurts, habits, or hungerings.

Clearly, the two key concepts in this lesson—what you think about yourself and what God thinks about you—are related.

What do you think about yourself?

Your identity—how you think and feel about yourself—is shaped and misshaped throughout your early childhood and adolescence. Of course, identity is not based on one single factor, but always on a whole constellation of influences as well as one's natural, God-given temperament.

The diagram illustrates how one's identity is formed.

I was taught how to feel about myself by my experiences, family, friends, society, etc. So

I feel a certain way about myself, and

I see the world in terms of that feeling and

I respond to the world that I see in ways that

lead to consequences that may reinforce the way I feel about myself and others.

Mirrors That Distort

Whenever we rely on other people's responses to us to give us an idea of who we are, we are likely to encounter warped mirrors. Do you remember the amusement park mirrors that distort the way you look, giving you the illusion of being fat or thin, short or tall? People and events in our lives can distort our internal identity in the same way. As a result, our view of ourselves is not always accurate.

Consider the three factors discussed below. The first two impact us on the unconscious level, and have their roots in our infancy and adolescence. We deal with the third factor on the conscious level and, by God's grace, find ourselves able to break free of false ideas about ourselves that we learned from warped mirrors. This step becomes possible in adulthood and is essential to having a truly adult faith.

FACTOR #1 — YOU LEARN TO MEET OTHER PEOPLE'S EXPECTATIONS.
Motivated by the rewards and punishments meted out by external authorities, you strive to gain approval and avoid disapproval.

 When has this factor affected you? Share a specific example or two.

FACTOR #2 — CERTAIN PEOPLE SET PATTERNS WHICH YOU IMITATE.
You strive to please significant authority figures—the parents, teachers, pastors, coaches, friends, and peer groups in your life.

 When has this factor affected you? Again, share a specific example or two.

Sadly, none of us grew up in a perfect environment or was raised by parents who perfectly modeled the character of God. As a result, each of us enters adulthood with a self-concept that is based at least in part upon our achievements, the recognition they bring us, and the approval we receive from our parents and significant others. We learn to accept ourselves only if we live up to certain expectations, and we learn not to accept ourselves unless others accept us. (We'll see at Milestone #6 that our three enemies—the world, the flesh, and the devil—are the forces behind the warped mirrors that teach us these unhealthy lessons.)

Learning to meet other people's expectations and striving to imitate the behavior of significant authority figures predisposes us to justify ourselves or condemn ourselves.

• First, when we learn that acceptance must be earned, we either lower our standards and expectations or we improve our performance. Both options invite self-justification, and self-justification works itself out in such things as self-atonement, perfectionism, competitiveness, comparing ourselves to others, pushing for achievement, making excuses for ourselves, and deviousness.

• Second, learning that failures result in punishment, we learn to condemn ourselves. This self-condemnation leads us to believe that God disapproves of us and that we are ineligible for His love. We develop an overly sensitive conscience, and we may act out our feelings of shame—our sense that we are unacceptable and worthless—by being self-effacing and unassertive.

In what circumstances do you find yourself justifying your actions or feelings? What circumstances prompt you to condemn yourself? Be specific.

Seeing Yourself as God Sees You

What does God think about you? Milestone #1 will help you put yourself in a position where God can reshape your self-concept so that it is based on the truth of what He thinks about you. God is holy and morally perfect (1 John 1:5), and He knows all our sin and darkness. Yet He fully and irreversibly forgives us that sin. Knowing who you are in relation to this gracious God and trusting in His unchanging and unconditional love for you—that is the only sure foundation for a healthy identity.

Replacing the Warped Mirrors

Remember that Factors #1 and #2 were external forces that affected you without you being aware of their impact. Factor #3, the factor we deal with on a conscious level, enables us to break free of the false, inaccurate, and damaging ideas about ourselves that we learned from warped mirrors.

FACTOR #3 — I CHOOSE TO BELIEVE AND LIVE ACCORDING TO THE TRUTH OF GOD'S LOVE FOR ME.
Your conscious decision is key: You now choose to think about yourself as God thinks about you. You choose to confirm the value God has ascribed to you. Your salvation is assured. You are not unacceptable, unworthy, or insignificant! You are not ineligible for His love. Because of Jesus' blood and if you have named Jesus as your Savior and Lord, God totally accepts you, you are worthy of His love, and you are significant in His sight. You are eligible for His love, and His love is relentless, reliable, and restorative. You need not labor to invent a new self that other people will admire or that will somehow be acceptable to our holy God. You can also take off masks, discard pretense, and risk being open and honest with God and other people. God will do a work of renewal in your life as you look deeply into two transforming mirrors: salvation and identity.

A Transforming Mirror: Your Salvation is Guaranteed

When you gaze intently at the truth that God fully forgives your sins, He will use that truth to renew your identity. As a result, you will increasingly see yourself as God sees you. Furthermore, as a Christian, you can be certain of your salvation. In the original Greek of 1 John 2:12, the verb "are... forgiven" teaches that you were forgiven in the past when Jesus died on the cross for your sins and that this forgiveness remains in the present. We believers can travel far on the journey of faith knowing that forgiveness is absolute, unconditional, undeserved, and nonrepayable. This unexpected miracle of mercy means that salvation and eternal life are guaranteed. The following statement can help you internalize this truth. Take the time to absorb it:

My salvation is certain and secure. God accepts me completely. So I will stop trying to bargain with God and working to earn God's grace. Instead, I will choose to rest in His unconditional grace.

 Comment on the following two statements. What does each one mean to you personally?

"By forgiving us completely, God obligates us to forgive ourselves—and makes it sin for us not to."

"Launch out in reckless trust that the redemption is complete... and bother no more about yourself."

Find Out For Yourself

The Bible clearly teaches that an intimate relationship with God and the divine repair which He offers His children are the result of His nonrepayable forgiveness and His unearned love for you.

 What does each of the following verses teach you about the certainty of God's love and forgiveness? Put an ✕ next to one passage that gives you greater assurance of your salvation. Explain your selection.

John 3:36   **1 John** 5:12-13

5:24

6:37, 39

10:27-29

Other verses reassure us of God's love and forgiveness. Take time to read some of th0se: Romans 5:1-2; 8:1; and 8:31-39; Colossians 2:13-15; and Hebrews 10:14, 17, 23.

 Why is the assurance of God's forgiveness and love essential to an intimate and ever-deepening relationship with Him? Try to give three reasons.

If a Christian isn't secure in God's love or confident about His forgiveness, what impact might that insecurity or lack of confidence have on his/her spiritual life? on life in general?

 In your personal experience, does God's love ever seem to diminish? If so, when and why?

A Transforming Mirror: Your Identity as God's Son/Daughter

Replace the warped, distorting mirrors with the transforming mirror of God's truth that you are loved, secure, and significant as His child. Choose to see yourself as God sees you. Enjoy your privileged status and immeasurable worth as a son or daughter of God. In 1 John 2:12, we are called "little children," a term of endearment and affection (2:1; 3:1-2,10; 5:2). In 3:1-2, even though the apostle John was over ninety years old, he still marveled at the extent of God's mercy and at his worth as God's son. Like John, as we age and mature in our faith, we can continue to marvel at God's gracious acceptance and love and, as a result, more easily admit our tendency to condemn ourselves, justify ourselves, and fashion protective masks of pretense. Instead of investing energy in those fruitless efforts, we can choose to trust in the strong and persistent love of God. Ask Him to help you absorb that truth, expressed in the following statement:

> I'm loved, secure, and significant as God's child. Because He loves me and forgives me, I can and I will learn to love and forgive myself. After all, I am a son/daughter of God!

So what does God think about you? First and foremost, He loves you unconditionally — not in spite of your sins and faults, but even though He is very aware of them! And God's love for you is causeless (you've done nothing to earn or deserve it), ceaseless (He loved you before you were born and He'll never stop loving you), and measureless (try to get your mind around that amazing and wonderful truth!). In Christ, you are forgiven, worthy, and secure in God's love. You can let go of any destructive sense of inferiority or superiority and let God bless you with the freedom to be real and the healing to be complete. You can replace the mirrors that distort how you see yourself and instead look into the transforming mirrors of truths of salvation and identity that God holds up to you. Shatter those old mirrors that reflect lies and illusions. Dare to believe and live by God's truth!

 8 Imagine basing your significance and worth on your identity as God's son/daughter. What is one practical difference that new way of thinking would make in your life?

Pilgrim in Progress

A Christian's growing faith is based on both content and process. We've looked at the biblical content of faith. The Scriptures clearly teaches that, as a Christian, you are a child in God's care. You are fully forgiven, unconditionally loved, and immeasurably worthy.

When you choose to accept the content of your faith, you begin the process of spiritual growth and transformation— the lifelong process of becoming who you are in Christ. This process involves affirming for yourself again and again who you are in Christ, thereby reprogramming the false ways of thinking about yourself that are based on distorted ideas. Working in partnership with the Holy Spirit to overhaul your identity, you will need to discard a self-concept based on performance and merit. Let Him reshape and redefine your identity based on God's unconditional love for you.

Hear what one fellow pilgrim says about the fundamental issues of the first milestone of the faith—and be encouraged! In *Knowing God*, J.I. Packer writes:

> What matters supremely, therefore, is not, in the last analysis, the fact that I know God, but the larger fact which underlies it—the fact that He knows me. I am graven on the palms of His hands; I am never out of His mind. All my knowledge of Him depends on His sustained initiative in knowing me. I know Him because He first knew me and continues to know me. He knows me as a friend... There is tremendous relief in knowing that His love to me is utterly realistic based at every point on prior knowledge of the worst about me, so that no discovery can now disillusion Him about me. [2]

A Closing Prayer

Almighty God, what a privilege to call you "Father"... and to be fully accepted as Your son/daughter... I thank You for Your restorative grace, Your relentless love, and Your reliable forgiveness... I ask You to free me from any pretense by which I attempt to defend my sin and hide my inadequacies.... I am loved, even though I know the ways in which I am unlovely. I am secure and safe in You, and I thank You as I pray in the name of Your Son who died for me so that I might be Your child. Amen.

Lesson 3

Milestone #1 Experiencing Grace and Forgiveness
Part 2

The Childhood Stage:
The Birth of Faith

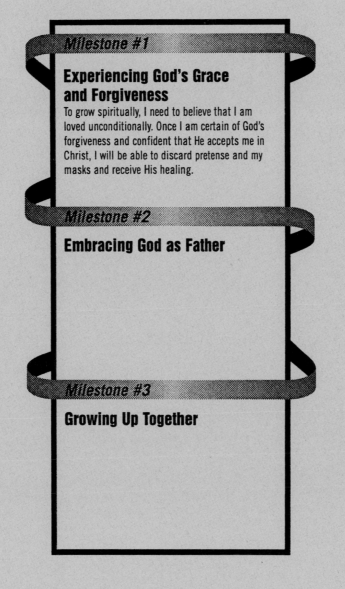

Milestone #1

Experiencing God's Grace and Forgiveness

To grow spiritually, I need to believe that I am loved unconditionally. Once I am certain of God's forgiveness and confident that He accepts me in Christ, I will be able to discard pretense and my masks and receive His healing.

Milestone #2

Embracing God as Father

Milestone #3

Growing Up Together

God's grace challenges you to boldly face the lie that says you are ineligible for His love. It will take courage for you to candidly walk in the light of that truth and to honestly admit to God your hurts, your needs, your failures, and the enormity of your self-centeredness. It will take humility to extend your tired, empty hands and receive God's gift of unconditional love, a gift that you don't deserve and can't ever repay. But by God's grace you can learn to stand strong in His grace and let Him love you – faults, forgiven sins, and all!

As you open yourself to receiving God's great love, be aware that five clouds can veil and conceal His grace. These clouds, the topic of this lesson, slow a Christian's spiritual growth.

Aims of Lesson #3

Plan to spend about two hours completing this lesson and preparing for your small-group time. During your time of personal study, you will:

◆ Review the truths of Lesson #2
◆ Look at key Bible passages in order to identify the clouds that can obstruct a life based on clearly seeing God's grace
◆ Consider how God offers healing grace where there has been pain and suffering.

For Small-Group Leaders:

We recommend that during the ninety-minute study portion of this meeting, group members discuss the following questions.

Lesson 3
1-7

You will not be able to give equal time to each question. So, as the group leader, budget your time carefully.

☑ Note:

Before reading through this Milestone, take a moment to glance at your **Spiritual Growth Profile**. Looking briefly at that mirror to your spiritual journey will help you put the coming discussion into the more personal context of your own spiritual growth.

Although *grace* is a familiar word, we tend to talk about it more often than we experience it. In order to truly know God's grace, each of us needs to embrace biblical principles of a grace-based life, principles that can help us open ourselves to His restorative and transforming touch. Learning to live in God's grace and choosing to receive the divine healing He offers us are two essentials to becoming more and more the new creations we are in Christ. Even if you have been a Christian for many years, the truths of Milestone #1 can bring refreshment and renewal—if you will risk making those truths your own.

Retracing Our Steps

As we've seen, the Childhood stage of faith is comprised of three milestones. Milestone #1 addresses the renewal of your self-concept or identity; Milestone #2, the renewal of your concept of God; and Milestone #3, the renewal of your relationships. This divine curriculum for the Childhood stage of faith—that we revisit throughout life—enriches your walk of faith and deepens your relationship with God and others.

Know here at the outset, however, that neglecting or overlooking Milestone #1 will delay and even cripple your spiritual growth. Until you have let God's Word and His Spirit correct your view of yourself, your progress toward each of the other seven milestones will be negatively impacted. To ensure healthy spiritual growth, let the Holy Spirit help you shatter the distorted mirrors that have warped your true identity in Christ. Your spiritual health depends on it!

 Again, the first milestone in the stages of faith is to experience God's grace and forgiveness. The milestone is based on the statement in 1 John 2:12—"I am writing to you, little children, because your sins are forgiven you for His name's sake." Your relationship with God is to become increasingly rooted in both your assurance of salvation ("I'm fully forgiven!") and your confidence in your status as a son/daughter in Christ ("I'm loved, secure, and significant!").

 **Moving Away From...** Milestone #1 involves the process of moving away from dys-grace and toxic faith—from your sense that you are ineligible for God's love and forgiveness; from self-condemnation and self-justification; from being motivated by reward and punishment; from performing to please, and an addiction to approval; from the legalism and tyranny of "ought"; from pretense; and from shame-based living that sabotages our adult lives.

 **Moving Toward...** At the same time that you move away from dys-grace and toxic faith in Milestone #1, you will move toward grace-based living—toward reprogramming your thinking about yourself based on God's grace and truth; toward finding security and significance as a son/daughter of God; toward confidence in God's certain, unconditional, and nonrepayable love; and toward experiencing divine healing of any crippling hurts, habits, or hungerings.

The Path of Grace

Your relationship with God is based on discovering and experiencing His grace. In fact, your journey of faith begins only when you choose to rely entirely on His grace for life in the present and for eternal life (Romans 5:1; Ephesians 2:8-9; Titus 3:7). From that point on, your gradual transformation toward Christlikeness will also happen by God's grace. His amazing, restorative grace is always unconditional, undeserved, unmerited, and nonrepayable! Spiritual growth will flourish when we are "strong in the grace that is in Jesus" (2 Timothy 2:1); "it is good for the heart to be strengthened by grace" (Hebrews 13:9). It is no wonder that believers are encouraged to "keep yourselves in the love of God" (Jude 21).

How often, however, we shift over—and we don't even do so consciously—to thinking that our relationship with God is conditional. We begin to think and act as if our relationship with Him is based on performing and pleasing Him as well as others. We live out the thoughts that "I am loved if..."; "I am loved when..."; and "I am loved because..." Regretfully, we can "*nullify* the grace of God" (Galatians 2:21, emphasis added) and "*insult* the Spirit of grace" (Hebrews 10:29, emphasis added). After all, the world, the flesh, and the devil (the three arch enemies we'll discuss in Milestone #6) have programmed us to base our identity and worth on our performance and on other people's opinions of us.

Deaf to Grace

In Matthew 18:23-35, Jesus tells a powerful story about grace, guilt, and debt-collecting. As you read this story about an unmerciful servant, realize that he had accumulated an unbelievably massive debt too big to pay back. One silver talent was worth 6,000 days wages for the average worker, so ten thousand talents was worth roughly 60 million days wages. To our amazement, the owner of the servant graciously forgave and canceled this entire debt (verse 27). What an incredible gift! The servant had just won the lottery!

What follows, however, is equally amazing and potentially quite convicting. Notice that verse 28 begins with the word *but*. Apparently the servant didn't completely understand the significance of his debt being cancelled. After all, we see him immediately and ruthlessly force others to repay what they owed him, debts that were much smaller than what he himself had owed. Too often we, like the bankrupt slave, are just as deaf when it comes to truly hearing God's extravagant and amazing grace. How can this be? And what can we do about it?

Five Clouds That Obstruct Grace

Along the journey of faith, we Christians encounter clouds that keep us from clearly seeing and fully experiencing God's grace. These clouds can interfere with His healing and renewing work is us. The following passages identify five such clouds that can conceal God's grace. Think about each one and record your answers to the questions.

Cloud #1 — Within the Self. Review Matthew 18:26-28 and Luke 15:18-19 ("I am no longer worthy to be called your son."). Our twisted, sinful nature keeps us from receiving and resting in God's restoring grace and His healing forgiveness. Guilt, shame, self-condemnation, and self-justification diminish our personal transformation. Also, it is our nature to both magnify our flaws and discount our strengths, a tendency that further blinds us to God's grace.

 What evidence do you see that this cloud within yourself has affected your experience of God's grace?

Cloud #2 — In the Church. Read Colossians 2:6-8, 20-23. The church can be home for legalistic moralizers, and it can emphasize externals and duty as a means to merit God's grace. Such codified rules and conformity to "oughts" and "shoulds" will veil the Lord's grace. Also, believers may have been taught that they can lose their salvation, or that it can be preserved by their efforts, or that some "second blessing" or experience is proof of their relationship with God. But note that each of these faulty teachings makes salvation a prize to be earned, when salvation is always a gift, with no strings attached!

 Why do these "in the church" clouds conceal God's grace from people? Which of these clouds, if any, have interfered with your experience of God's grace? Explain.

Cloud #3— At Home. Look at Ephesians 6:4 and Colossians 3:21. We expect our parents and significant others to be trustworthy, and we count on them to provide care, nurturance, warmth, and affection. Instead they may bring dys-grace and shame by not treating us like God's beloved children, like the people of infinite worth that we are. Also, any rigid, rule-based approach to the Christian life clouds God's grace and His healing that brings wholeness. [1] When we're offered a set of rules to follow and told to call that "faith," we may grow up feeling unacceptable, unaccepted, and unworthy of God's love because we can't perfectly follow all the rules all the time. Faith becomes toxic when it holds forth rigid expectations that focus on external behaviors and performing to please.

When, if ever, have you experienced this "at home" cloud interfering with your spiritual growth? Explain.

Cloud #4 — In Culture. Read Mark 4:19; Romans 12:2; and 1 Corinthians 1:20. You may have felt scorned by and unacceptable to those very people you most wanted and even needed to accept you. You may have felt the shame of being rejected by your own group. The message you heard was "You don't measure up. You have to be the way others want you to be." You worked tirelessly to be noticed, to belong, and fit in. Now, if you, as an adult, base your worth and acceptance on people you deem significant, this cloud will obstruct God's grace.

 How has this "culture cloud" stood in the way of your seeing God's grace? Explain.

Cloud #5 — In High Places. In Revelation 12:10, the devil is described as the "accuser of the brethren," a phrase that exposes Satan's dark strategy to interfere with and slow down the believer's journey. Satan relies on accusation and deception to obstruct the believer's progress, and we too easily believe Satan's lies, rather than the truth of God's Word. The devil would have us believe that our sin is unforgivable, salvation cannot be guaranteed, and God's love is conditional.

 What evidence of Satan successfully blocking your spiritual growth do you find in your life?

Healing Grace

Grace allows you to accept God's love and to rest in the truth that, in Christ, you are worthy of that love. God's grace frees you from the performing and people-pleasing by which you have tried to earn acceptance. You are not inadequate and defective! Rather, God sees you as forgiven in Jesus, and He totally accepts you. He even adopts you into His family! God's grace frees you to live openly in His love, to experience transparent friendships that you've never before known, and to receive His healing for your hidden wounds. Let Him love you!

Grace also means that you are free to discard masks and pretense. You can come out from behind the protective walls you've built around yourself. Whether you have been abused, shamed, neglected, driven to perfectionism, or are ashamed of your past—whatever your story and whatever your hurts, habits, or hungerings—let God love you with His healing, renewing, and hope-filled love! Furthermore, God's grace challenges you to boldly face the lie that you are ineligible for His love. God's grace challenges you to let His love deliver you from painful memories, cleanse you of fermenting resentments, and set you free from their shackles and infections! God's grace brings divine restoration!

Milestone #1 is about celebrating God's curative grace! When you truly experience God's acceptance of you—when this first of the three parts of the guardrail is firmly in place—you will be able to travel far in your faith! And you will know great joy!

Readiness for the Milestone #1

Although children and youth can personally experience God's love and grace, achieving a stable identity is beyond the capability of even most high-school adolescents. After all, adolescents are in flux as they begin to shed their fixation on self and start dealing with the identity questions that require the abstract thinking ability necessary for identity formation. Nor are adolescents governed by the internal, self-chosen principles (such as Factor #3 in the previous lesson) that would enable them to move beyond the need to both conform to significant others and win their peers' approval. The ability to apply moral principles to a wide range of daily decisions is still quite undeveloped even in sixteen year-olds. The ability to clearly and solidly identify yourself as a child of God and to live free of all the defenses and false ideas you learned growing up is central to an adult faith, and that ability will come as you work on this milestone. Of course, you'll be experiencing God's grace and forgiveness throughout your lifetime.

Pilgrim in Progress

In these first two lessons, we've looked at Milestone #1, "Experiencing God's Grace and Forgiveness." Know that throughout your life you will be dealing with this matter of identity-formation, with seeing yourself as a beloved child of God, and with the need for God's healing teach.

 What is one area of your life that you will open up to God's gracious strengthening and/or healing power?

Your Guide: The Mentoring Parent

As you work on each of the eight milestones, you will benefit from the insight and experience of one who has already traveled this road before you. Such a Parent in the faith would be well acquainted with this critical first milestone. A Parent in the faith will have firmly established his/her identity in Christ, will be able to see beyond the clouds that obstruct grace, will have experienced God's healing touch, and will therefore be qualified to share his/her story and to help you your spiritual journey.

 Who already is—or might be—a Parent in the faith to you? Ask God to bring such a person into your life if He hasn't already. A Young Adult in the faith can also be a worthy example to a Child in the faith. Seek out one or two fellow believers for support and accountability and who will challenge you to grow.

 What skills might a mentoring Parent need in order to help the Child in the faith who is working on Milestone #1? Try to list four.

1.

2.

3.

4.

A Closing Prayer

Thank You, God, for Your gift of grace.... and for the privilege of being Your son/daughter.... Please help me to live out that truth and to experience the freedom that comes with Your unconditional love.... Give me the courage to come out from behind walls I've built... to experience Your healing touch... and to let a Parent or Young Adult come alongside me in my journey of faith.... I pray in the name of Your precious Son, my Savior. Amen.

Milestone #2 Embracing God as Father

The Childhood Stage:
The Birth of Faith

Milestone #1

Experiencing Grace and Forgiveness

To grow spiritually, I need to believe that I am loved unconditionally. Once I am certain of God's forgiveness and confident that He accepts me in Christ, I will be able to discard pretense and my masks and receive His healing.

Milestone #2

Embracing God as Father

To grow spiritually, I need to know God as my Father, as the One in whom I can trust and to whom I can surrender my life. In order to know God as Father, I will replace my distorted ideas of God with biblical truth about Him and then let my heavenly Father re-parent me.

Milestone #3

Growing Up Together

The second milestone of the Childhood stage of faith involves the renewal of your concept of God. Your perception and feelings about God arise from what you think God feels about you and are rooted in your experiences from childhood, adolescence, and even adulthood. In addition to looking at what you think God feels about you, you'll take some time to discover how your professed beliefs about God differ from your felt-sense of God. In other words, the God of your head may not match the God of your heart. During the tasks of this second milestone, you'll bring both the God of your head and the God of your heart into line with the God of the Bible.

Aims of Lesson #4

Plan to spend about two hours completing this lesson and preparing for your small-group time. During your time of personal study, you will:

- Trace the process by which you developed your concept of God
- Identify any connection between your life experiences and your current ideas and feelings about God
- Take a step away from distorted concepts of God and a step toward a more complete surrender to God and a greater trust in Him

Questions in this lesson may cause you a degree of discomfort. Be aware of those feelings and know that the discomfort may be telling you something about yourself. Also, feel free to concentrate on those issues that especially interest you or those that promise to be of most helpful to you. Finally, schedule some time each day this week to work on this lesson.

For Small-Group Leaders:

We recommend that during the ninety-minute study portion of this meeting, group members discuss the following questions:

Lesson 2
1-3, 5-8

You will not be able to give equal time to each question. So, as the group leader, budget your time carefully.

☑ Note:

Before reading through this Milestone, take a moment to glance at your **Spiritual Growth Profile**. Looking briefly at that mirror to your spiritual journey will help you put the coming discussion into the more personal context of your own spiritual growth.

At the first milestone in the Childhood stage of faith, you were encouraged to look at your concept of yourself, your identity. At this second milestone of Childhood, you'll deal with your concept of God and determine where your ideas are inaccurate, misleading, or even debilitating. Your concept of God has to do with what you think God feels about you. You may come to realize, if you haven't already, that your professed beliefs about God differ from your felt-sense of God.

Retracing Our Steps

At Milestone #1 you focused on God's grace and forgiveness and thought about how you have experienced them in your life. Therein lies the key to an adult's strong and growing faith. First, are you living free of guilt and shame, assured of your salvation and confident of the fact that you are fully forgiven? Also, is your sense of self rooted in your privileged status as a son/daughter of God who knows that you are loved, that you have significance in your heavenly Father's eyes, and that you can rest secure in His love?

A personal knowledge of God's grace and forgiveness means that your journey of faith is underway and that you are beginning to erect a guardrail essential for your lifelong travels. Your firsthand knowledge of God's grace also results in a renewal of your identity or self-concept. Challenged to shatter the mirrors that kept you from seeing yourself as God sees you, you can now begin to progress toward a life free of both pretense and the pressure to perform in order to be accepted.

Overview of Milestone #2
Embracing God as Father: A New Way of Relating to God

When you shatter any perceptions of God that distort your ability to see Him as your heavenly Father, and then when you are able to embrace Him as such, you can experience the renewal of your concept of God. That more accurate picture of the Lord of the Universe is the second part of the guardrail that will keep you on the path toward spiritual maturity and wholeness. As A.W. Tozer put it,

> Our real idea of God may lie buried under the rubbish of conventional religious notions and may require an intelligent and vigorous search before it is finally unearthed and exposed for what it is. Only after an ordeal of painful self-probing are we likely to discover what we actually believe about God. [1]

Based on John's statement in 1 John 2:13 ("I have written to you, children, because you know the Father"), Milestone #2 addresses the core issue of your concept of God. The goal is to be able to say and believe, "I am a trusting child of God, both bonded and surrendering to my heavenly Father by faith in His unconditional love and care."

Moving Away From... In Milestone #2, you will work on moving away from any faulty and distorted but persistent impressions about God that interfere with your relationship with Him. You will let go of a God you have made in your image and work to resolve any contradictions between the God of your head *and* the God of your heart and the God of the Bible.

Moving Toward... As you move away from your inaccurate understanding of God in Milestone #2, you will move toward a greater trust in God and the ultimate intimacy reflected by the title "Abba" ("Daddy"), which you as a believer are privileged to call Him. You will let your heavenly Father reparent you and, as a result, be able to more fully surrender your life to your heavenly Father.

Consider what the original Greek of 1 John 2:13 says. First, the word John used for children (*paidia*) refers to a very young and dependent child, not yet seven years old, who needs protection, training, guidance, and discipline. Second, the Greek word for *know* speaks of knowing something firsthand through personal experience. This knowledge goes beyond merely knowing about a certain something or someone. Finally, John refered to God as "the Father." We can trust our heavenly Parent without resistance, reluctance, or reservation. Perhaps in sharp contrast to our earthly father, God our heavenly Father is absolutely trustworthy, completely safe, and utterly reliable.

The words of the apostle John invite you to experience fellowship with this wonderful and holy Father (1 John 1:3; 2:20). Forgiven by God and accepted through Jesus Christ, we Christians can walk in intimate communion with our holy God, and we can do so without hesitation, apprehension, or fear. We can address our heavenly Father with perfect openness and honesty (1 John 1:5-10). Our God is not austere or exacting, so we need not hide from Him. Instead, our God is perfect Light and Love (1 John 1:5 and 4:8) and therefore a flawless Father for His sons and daughters. We can trust God completely and follow Him fully.

God the Father
A Radical Thought Then; A Neglected Truth Now

In Jesus' day, the name of God was so sacred that ordinary people were not even supposed to speak it. For centuries, in fact, the Jews had used the letters "YHWH" to refer to God, and only the High Priest could pronounce that word—and then only when he entered the Holy of Holies on the annual Day of Atonement. Readers of Scripture who came to these letters would say "Adonnai" ("Lord") instead of "Yahweh." When writing about God in Romans 8:15 and Galatians 4:6, however, Paul used *Abba*, the Aramaic term for "father" and one of the first words a child spoke (similar to our *papa* or *dada*). Likening our relationship with God to the relationship between a child and his/her daddy was abhorrent to an orthodox Jew. But on the cross, Jesus Christ bridged that unbridgeable chasm between God and human beings, and now we are free to address God as "Father."

As one theologian has observed, "There is one attribute of God through which we are able to see all the other facets of Him. It serves as a viewpoint from which we are able to view all the other facets of His personality. God is first and foremost, above and beyond anything else, a Father."

A Parable about Two Brothers

In Luke 15:11-32, Jesus painted an unforgettable portrait of God as Father as He told a powerful story about two brothers whose personal searches for meaning and a relationship with God takes radically different forms. [2] If you look closely, you will probably see yourself in both brothers.

The Younger Son: *Searching for Love Where It Cannot Be Found*

Read Luke 15:11-24. We are like this younger son every time we look for our needs to be met in places where they cannot be satisfied.

 Why do you think the younger son left home even though he had a good and generous father?

In "the distant country," the younger son came to his senses. Realizing that his rebellion had led only to emptiness and disillusionment, he decided to return home to the father. In what ways has this younger son's experience been your experience? Explain.

The Long Way Home

One of the greatest challenges to spiritual growth is learning to rest in both the Father's unconditional acceptance of us and our undeserved, unshakable status as His son or daughter. Expecting the father's love to be conditional, this son doubted whether he would even be welcome when he got home. Did you notice in Jesus' story that, as he headed for his home, the son practiced a speech (verses 17-19)? The son was willing to be treated as a hired servant rather than a forgiven child. As he was about to say, "I am no longer worthy to be called your son," the father interrupted the son's apology (verse 21) and welcomed him home with a great celebration.

 The prodigal son expected to be benched, to be treated as a second-string player, when he returned home. In what ways are you settling for being a hired servant, a second-string player in God's kingdom, rather than living joyfully as a forgiven and beloved son/daughter of your heavenly Father? Be specific.

Soul-Party

Luke 15:20-24 describes the homecoming. The father ran to his son and embraced him. Imagine the son's surprise as his father throws a party in honor of his return home. His father fully accepts him without reservation. Just as the father celebrated his love for his returning son, may you celebrate your heavenly Father's great love for you! In fact, go ahead and arrange your own joyous and festive soul-party! Choose to let go of any guilt you've felt about the past. You can fully trust your Father's graciousness and celebrate wholeheartedly, knowing that you have not disqualified yourself from receiving His undeserved love and absolute forgiveness. Fine tune a new script that emphasizes God's grace and mercy, a script that you rehearse often and then party hearty as you celebrate your identity as His son or daughter.

 Party often in your soul as you journey through life. And pause right now and take a few minutes now to enjoy simply being Home with your Father. At this soul-party, you'll find freedom and laughter and maybe some tears as you surrender yourself to His care.

The Older Brother: *Lost in Resentment*

Read Luke 15:25-32. Unlike the younger son, the older son has remained home, but not happily. This son is full of resentment, and anger. He had never left home with his inheritance. Instead, he had always been scrupulously dutiful about fulfilling his obligations. He was probably admired, respected, and considered a model son. Yet he was self-righteous, self-pitying, and jealous. In his heart, the older son was far from home and just as lost as his younger brother had been. Hear the whine: "I never received what was due me. I tried so hard to please you, I did so much around this place for you, and I still have not received what others have." [2]

 What was the older brother's underlying misconception about his father? (It may be similar to your underlying misconception about your heavenly Father!)

The father says to the older boy, "Son, you have always been with me, and all that is mine is yours" (verse 31). Why didn't the eldest son see and believe this truth? And why—if you do—do you struggle to accept your heavenly Father's loving presence with you and all the riches of His kingdom?

Realize that the father loved both sons and that he wanted to celebrate with both sons. He did not love the younger son more than he loved the elder—or vice versa. So, whether you see yourself as being more like the prodigal son or more like the older brother, you can return home to the Father whose unlimited and unconditional love will welcome you and even celebrate you. You truly can trust the Father's love.

Your Concept of God: What Is It?

Hear what William and Christi Gaultiere write in their book *Mistaken Identity*:

> Your God Image is the collection of emotional images of God that you have deep inside your heart. It's your private experience of relating to God. You might think of your God Image as your perception of God's attitudes toward you or the way that you feel He relates with you. These perceptions form a certain set of expectations about how God will treat you. Your God Image is the picture of God you draw inside your heart with the different colored crayons of your emotions... This perceptual concept of God is different than your professed beliefs about God.

Simply put, your God-concept has to do with what you feel God feels about you. The Gaultieres continue:

> For many of us, our image of God is like Dorothy and her friends' image of the Wizard of Oz. If you remember, Dorothy was lost in the land of Oz and was homesick for Kansas. The friends she met in the land of Oz also had some problems. The scarecrow needed a brain, the tin man needed a heart, and the lion wanted courage. They had been told that the Wizard of Oz was kind and wonderful and would give them their wishes. Filled with hope, they sang and skipped down the yellow brick road to the Emerald City. When they got there and met the Wizard, they were shocked by a horrifying and ugly monster on a huge screen blowing out smoke and thundering angry threats at them. The four of them trembled in fear before this image of a terrifying wizard.

> They had heard that the Wizard of Oz was so kind and wonderful and would help them, yet the Wizard they saw on the screen was so mean he cruelly turned them away without offering any help. It wasn't until Toto pulled open the curtain that they saw the real Wizard of Oz wasn't the one up on the screen. He was a kind old man who was gentle and caring. [3]

Like Dorothy and her traveling companions facing the image of the monstrous wizard, you may be relating to a mistaken caricature of God on the screen of your heart.

Your Concept of God: Its Source

Your concept of God is the cumulative result of your childhood, adolescent, and even adulthood experiences and your memories of those. Like your concept of yourself (see Milestone #1), your concept of God is shaped and misshaped by the influence of your relationships with significant others as well as by your unique life experiences. Furthermore, your personal interpretation of these events is a big factor in your experience of them. Simply put, your image of God is more caught by life's circumstances than formally taught by any book or teacher. It's no surprise, then, that each one of us has a concept of God that is distorted in some way.

Consider the ways in which the following five factors can contribute to a false image of God. [4]

A series of negative interactions with significant people in your life. Too often we conclude that God relates to us in the same negative way that we were treated by people who were supposed to love us. Jack couldn't do enough to please his father, and he never felt close to his mother. Susan was sexually abused by her uncle. Jason was repeatedly put down by his first-grade teacher in front of his peers. Understandably, all three struggle to trust God and be intimate with Him.

Mistaking the guilt-inducing condemnation of your conscience for the voice of God. Bill's legalistic brand of Christianity is very works oriented. Therefore, his felt-sense of God is that He is a demanding and perfectionistic drill sergeant barking out orders. Consequently, Bill constantly fights the feelings of inadequacy, guilt, and shame that have been programmed into his thinking. His primary emotion toward God is fear. Afraid of triggering God's anger, Bill is reluctant to venture too close to Him.

Ineffective religious teaching and training. Mary grew up in a church that preached primarily about sin, salvation, and separation from worldliness, and her parents would not permit her to go to movies or dances. In Mary's eyes, God is a killjoy, and life is to be endured rather than enjoyed. Likewise, Shawn never heard much about God's unconditional love, forgiveness, and grace. He also missed out on learning to be honest with God, himself, and others. Any "hidden curriculum" (what is not said about God) can powerfully influence our perceptions of Him.

Traumatic circumstances for which we blame God. Phil's theology didn't include pain and disappointment. So when a personal crisis struck, Phil found it difficult to see God as a supportive ally. He thought that God must be punishing him for some sin. Phil also couldn't admit his anger to God. He found himself wrestling with such issues as "How could a good God allow this to happen?" "Where is God when life hurts?" and "This wouldn't happen if God cared!"

Misinterpreting Scripture. All of us have preconceived ideas and beliefs that shape the way we read and interpret verses. (The four factors just listed guarantee that!) Slow to recognize and often slow to correct our preconceptions and misconceptions, we read Scripture in such a way that reinforces our distorted image of God. Consider Matthew 5:48, "You are to be perfect as your heavenly Father is perfect," a verse that can fuel neurotic perfectionism in some people. We can find other support for our own dysfunctions in the Bible, and such misreading further keeps us from knowing God as He really is.

 Which one or two of the five factors you've just read about have most influenced your concept of God? Be specific.

Resulting Spiritual Problems

Wrong concepts about God and feelings based on those wrong concepts lead to various kinds of spiritual problems. According to seminary professor, pastor, and counselor David Seamands, the following are among the most common: the inability to feel forgiveness; the inability to trust and surrender to God; intellectual questions and theological doubts; and problems with neurotic perfectionism. [5]

David Seamands goes on to write:

> Sometimes I ask people who are having a difficult time describing their God to draw a picture of Him. As you might imagine, I have an interesting collection of drawings. Several depict a huge eye which covers a whole page—God watching everything they do, waiting to catch them at some failure or wrongdoing. Others have drawn angry human faces or birds of prey with sharp beaks and talons. One young theological student said he couldn't draw very well but next time he'd bring a picture of his God.

> I was very curious about it. It happened to be the Christmas season and he bought a magazine with an artist's drawing of an extra large, angry, and demanding Scrooge sitting behind a desk, quill pen in hand with his debit-credit ledger before him. Standing in front of the desk facing Scrooge was small, terror-stricken Bob Cratchett. Pointing to Scrooge he explained, "That's God," and then to Cratchett, "That's me." And just think, this young seminarian made an A in his theology class! [6]

Like the seminary student, you and I may have learned certain biblical truths about God, but we nevertheless carry with us a defective felt-sense of who God is. In other words, the God of your head may be quite different from the God of your heart. Your professed, creedal beliefs about God may not match your image of God.

The Power of Parents

As you're undoubtedly aware, our parents can be positive and/or negative models of God for us. The following autobiographical account by Corrie Ten Boom and the corresponding questions can help you identify the source of your concept of God. In this passage, Miss Ten Boom shows how parents can be positive models: her father taught her about God's gentle care, His steadfast love, and the security she could find in Him.

> My security was assured as a child. Every night I would go to the door of my room in my nightie and call out, "Papa, I'm ready for bed." He would come to my room and pray with me before I went to sleep. I can always remember that he took time with us and would tuck the blankets around my shoulders very carefully, with his own characteristic precision. Then he would put his hand gently on my face and say, "Sleep well, Corrie. I love you."

> I would be very, very still, because I thought that if I moved I might somehow lose the touch of his hand; I wanted to feel it until I fell asleep.

> Many years later in a concentration camp in Germany, I sometimes remembered the feeling of my father's hand on my face. When I was lying beside Betsie on a wretched, dirty mattress in that dehumanizing prison, I would say "Oh Lord, let me feel Your hand upon me.... May I creep under the shadow of Your wings." [7]

6 In what positive ways did your parents model who God is? Be specific.

Now consider what your parents may have done to present you with a negative model of God. Perhaps your parents were verbally abusive, unloving, absent, preoccupied, inaccessible, inattentive, emotionally distant, physically abusive, perfectionistic, impossible to please, demanding, manipulative, or condemning. Or, conversely, maybe your parents were doting, pampering, indulging, overly protective, or yielding; or perhaps they suffocated you with excessive attention and concern. Imagine the possible side effects qualities like these might have on the way a Christian relates to God!

 7 As you were growing up, what did you need in or from a parent but never received?

Replacing Distortions with Truth

The questions you've been answering may have brought to the surface some childhood pain. You may have touched on hurts that have long been buried and silent. You may also be surprised to discover how similar you are to either the younger son or the older brother in Jesus' story. So what will you do about the memories that caused you pain today? What will you do about the inaccurate image of God that keeps you in the role of the searching son or joyless older brother? The answer to those questions is to turn to your heavenly Father and choose to accept His unrepayable forgiveness, to receive the healing He offers you, and to enjoy His celebration of you, His very own son or daughter. Trust in the truth of God's Word to bring you wholeness and joy.

A quick disclaimer... Know that however healthy a person's concept of God is, the world, the flesh, and the devil conspire to distort it. After all, these enemies of spiritual growth want to jeopardize our spiritual growth at every point possible. The world, the flesh, and the devil take aim at your concept of God by offering compelling pictures of defective gods. (Refer to the bottom of page 34 for some false concepts of God.)

If you are a parent, consider what your children's sense of God might be like based on their unique life experience and the kind of parenting they are receiving from you. If you aren't a parent, think about someone you know and how the parenting he/she received may have influenced his/her concept of God.

> ## Readiness for the Milestone #2
> Your concept of God, and your mistaken beliefs about Him are formed as a result of your relationships and experiences throughout our lives. In order to develop a healthy adult faith, you need to recognize and revise any distorted images, misconceptions, or caricatures of God that are influencing you. You also need to challenge and discard any myths you are holding onto as truth. In adulthood, you are uniquely prepared to do this kind of work. Like Toto, you will be able to pull back the screen and see God for who He is. Then, for the rest of your life, you will be on a journey of rich discoveries as you see more and more clearly who your loving and faithful God really is.

Your Guide: The Mentoring Parent

At each step of your spiritual journey, you will benefit from the insight and experience of one who has already traveled before you. Such a Parent in the faith will have worked through Milestone #2 and will be embracing God as his/her heavenly Father. Having a renewed and biblical concept of God and being able to trust in the heavenly Father, the Parent is qualified to both share his/her personal story and guide you on your spiritual journey. A Young Adult in the Faith can also serve as a valuable example.

Pilgrim in Progress

 What specific thing will you begin to do to let God be your heavenly Parent, to trust Him more completely, or to more fully surrender yourself and your life to Him?

A Closing Prayer

Almighty God, You know—perhaps better than I—the ways I fail to see who You really are. You know that I see you as [share your distorted ideas about God].... Help me to let go of these false and distorted ideas. Teach me to believe that You are instead a God who loves me, a God who runs to meet me, and a God who celebrates my return Home. Home is where I want to stay. I believe, God. Please help my unbelief so that I may grow to know You better... so that I may fully embrace You as my heavenly Father. In Jesus' name. Amen.

J. B. Phillips noted some common distorted concepts of God

• Heavenly Policeman - God exists only to enforce broken laws. • Celestial Parent - Psychological guilt and fears are projected from earthly guardians onto God. • Bearded Grandfather - The Sovereign One is not only visualized as old but old-fashioned and weak. • Meek-and-Mild - God, through distorted images of Jesus, is pictured as soft and sentimental. • Absolute Perfection - God cannot accept anything less than 100 percent perfection from people. • Blissful Escape - Serving God takes the form of spiritual thumb sucking, providing a way to evade life s responsibilities. • God-in-a-Box - Idiosyncrasies of believers claim to cage the Creator (i.e. denominational exclusivity). • Transcendent Commander-in-Chief - When compared to the universe s vastness, it is preposterous to believe that God cares about individuals. • Media-mutilated Being - Most of the lies people are told about God are colorized by misrepresentations in the media. • Perennial Disappointment - Whether through unanswered prayer or undeserved disaster, he is the One who lets people down. • Pale Galilean - God is primarily a negative force in the lives of believers; they reduce spirituality to legalistic restrictions. • God-in-Our-Image - God is merely an extension of private expectations: God hates things that "others" do, yet he overlooks personal transgressions. • Time-Server - Like a hurried executive, the Father is driven by the clock. • Eternal Elitist - God is a respect of persons, favoring the privileged. • Sinai Superior - Old Testament commandments are valued over New Testament principles; the God of works over the God of grace. • Impersonal Power - God actually represents ultimate values; an enlightened form of rationalism. • Gods of Other Names. The Creator is linked with "gods" of fame, fortune, and success. [8]

In *The Subtle Power of Spiritual Abuse,* David Johnson and Jeff Van Vonderen list these misconceptions about God:

• A God who is never satisfied, who keeps setting higher and higher goals and is eager to let you find out how much you have missed the mark. • A mean, vindictive God, who is waiting for us to make a mistake. Then He is able to do what He would rather do anyway, which is to point out all our failures, or to punish and humiliate. • An apathetic God who watches when people are hurt and abused, but does nothing to help because it would mean having to challenge an authority figure or structure. • A God who is asleep and does not notice even when people are hurt and abused. • A God who is awake, close, and who sees and cares, but is powerless to help when people are hurt and abused. • A God who is a kind and fickle baby. His mood can be manipulated by our slightest mistake. • The "utterly holy God." He is like a spiritual burglar alarm, ready to go off any time you think about sin. [9]

Lesson 5

Milestone #3 Growing Up Together
Part 1

The Childhood Stage:
The Birth of Faith

Milestone #1

Experiencing God's Grace and Forgiveness

To grow spiritually, I need to believe that I am loved unconditionally. Once I am certain of God's forgiveness and confident that He accepts me in Christ, I will be able to discard pretense and my masks and receive His healing.

Milestone #2

Embracing God as Father

To grow spiritually, I need to know God as my Father, as the One in whom I can trust and to whom I can surrender my life. In order to know God as Father, I will replace my distorted ideas of God with biblical truth about Him and then let my heavenly Father re-parent me.

Milestone #3

Growing Up Together

To grow spiritually, I need to experience the mutually supportive and challenging relationships that can be found in the family of God. After all, we who are God's children grow whole when we're in community, not in isolation. We really do need one another.

The third milestone of Childhood targets the development of distinctively Christian relationships, the horizontal dimension of our faith. The whole of the New Testament places a weighty emphasis on the kind of personal relationships that are to characterize God's people, and these relationships are key to our ongoing spiritual growth.

Aims of Lesson #5

Plan on spending about two hours completing this lesson and preparing for your small-group time. During your time of personal study, you will:

◆ Consider the strengths and weaknesses of your relationships
◆ Identify obstacles to building community
◆ Develop a more adequate theology of Christian community (koinonia)

For Small-Group Leaders:

We recommend that during the ninety-minute study portion of this meeting, group members discuss the following questions.

Lesson 5
3-6, 8

You will not be able to give equal time to each question. So, as the group leader, budget your time carefully.

☑ Note:

Before reading through this Milestone, take a moment to glance at your **Spiritual Growth Profile**. Looking briefly at that mirror to your spiritual journey will help you put the coming discussion into the more personal context of your own spiritual growth.

The third milestone of Childhood emphasizes a **new way of relating to other people**. After all, having gained a healthier concept of God and a more accurate concept of yourself based on the fact that you are a much-loved child of God, you can now enter into richer, more intimate and more rewarding relationships with other people, relationships in which believers are like iron sharpening iron, spurring one another's growth toward Christlikeness.

Retracing Our Steps

The first two milestones of Childhood encouraged you to develop the Jesus-and-Me vertical dimension of your faith. Milestone #1 invited you to stop trying to earn God's acceptance and love and to instead live a life based on His gracious and unconditional acceptance of you. Milestone #2 challenged you to examine and revise your distorted ideas about God so that, again, you can live freely in His grace and love. Now, with Milestone #3, you move from the vertical dimension of your faith to the Jesus-and-We horizontal dimension, from the personal to the interpersonal.

The graphic above illustrates that both the vertical and horizontal dimensions of your faith are important to your spiritual health in the Childhood stage of faith. Two aspects of this interrelatedness of our identity in

Christ and our intimacy with others are worth noting. First of all, a solid understanding of our identity in Christ precedes genuine intimacy with His people. The health of our relationships results from our knowledge that, in Christ, we are forgiven, significant, and worthy. When you let God love you deeply, you can then love others deeply (1 John 4:10,11,19; 2 Corinthians 5:14). When you experience God's grace, you can extend His grace to others (Ephesians 4:29; 1 Peter 4:9). At the same time, however, our identity is realized in intimacy. Deep, caring relationships serve as the context in which our renewed Christian identity can be affirmed. God's love and forgiveness become real to us when people love us deeply. Without such intimacy, we cannot fully experience an identity renewed by God's grace and truth.

 Think about identity and intimacy in your own life. When has feeling better about yourself (identity) enabled you to be more accepting of others (intimacy)?

When has being accepted and loved by others (intimacy) helped you be more accepting of yourself (identity)?

The apostle John wrote, "What we have seen and heard we proclaim to you also, that you also may have fellowship with us; and indeed our fellowship is with the Father, and with His Son Jesus Christ" (1 John 1:3). True joy (1:4) results when we experience a faith rich in the vertical as well as in the horizontal dimension.

Overview of Milestone #3
Growing Up Together: A New Way of Relating to Others

The apostle John knew how important our relationships with other people are to our journey toward Christlikeness and spiritual maturity. Both our concept of self and our concept of God are experienced and reinforced in community. Tragically, the "Jesus & We" aspect of the spiritual life is too often neglected. People ignore the truth that relationships are powerfully linked to spiritual progress. In fact, relationships can either trigger spiritual growth or impair it. In Milestone #3, therefore, you will focus on your relationships with other people. Each of us can be reshaped in and by the grace-based family of God. Each of us can continue to grow spiritually as we extend God's grace and unconditional love to one another.

Based on the apostle John's statements: "I am writing to you, little children [*teknia*]" in 1 John 2:12, "brethren" (3:14), "one another" (3:11), and "beloved" (4:7)—Milestone #3 offers you a new awareness of the importance of relationships. This new perspective is based on the fact that we are all *teknia* whether we are in the Childhood, Young Adulthood, or Parenthood stage of faith. In Milestone #3, then, we focus on developing mutually supportive and challenging relationships in which we are committed to one another's spiritual growth and wholeness.

Moving Away From... In Milestone #3, you will work on moving away from superficial, detached, impoverished, and unhealthy relationships. You will work on moving away from relationships of proximity, relationships that lack real community. (In Western cultures, such unhealthy relationships are often characterized by self-sufficiency and anonymity. People in Eastern cultures, however, are often overly dependent on family and friends, and that can also lead to unhealthy relationships.)

Moving Toward... As you move away from unhealthy relationships, you will be moving toward relationships characterized by an empowering mix of support and challenge. You'll experience "group grace"; a sense of truly belonging; collaborative care; interdependence; and efforts to ensure each person's wholeness in Christ. A special place exists for mentoring Parents in such a matrix of relationships.

Partners in Progress

The apostle John stated very clearly that he wrote his epistle so "that you too may have fellowship [*koinonia*] with us" (1 John 1:3). *Koinonia* means "sharing your life in common with." For instance, Luke uses the word *koinonia* to describe the business partnership between the two pairs of brothers James and John and Andrew and Simon. As joint owners of a little fishing fleet, they were colleagues, engaged together in the fishing trade and committed to developing a successful business together. *Koinonia* is also used to describe the mutuality and intimacy of a marriage relationship. In authentic biblical *koinonia*, the people in relationship to one another are partners in spiritual progress, committed to empowering one another toward maturity and further Christlikeness.

John Stott has this to say about *koinonia*:

> There are two ideas of the religious life. There is the tramcar idea and the fireside idea. In the tramcar you sit beside your fellow-passenger. You are all going in the same direction, but you have no fellowship... Then there is the fireside, where the family meets together, where they are at home, where they converse one with another of common pursuits and common interests, and where a common relationship binds all together in a warm bond of love and fellowship.... And when we concentrate on this, we are no longer facing in the same direction, we are gathered in a circle, facing each other. [1]

2 Consider your relationships. Which are tramcar relationships?

What fireside relationships are you blessed with? Describe the good that they bring to your life.

When John called the recipients of his letter "little children" (2:12), a term of endearment, he was referring to Christians who are in close, caring relationships with him and with one another. Such kinship is essential to spiritual growth. We Christians are to be brothers and sisters to one another, able to both give and receive support and challenge.

My Life in Community

Each of us must regularly take a hard look at our relationships to be sure that they are adequate to fuel our journey of faith, and the following exercise serves as a good diagnostic tool for doing so. The eight Bible verses teach about the kind of relationships essential to our spiritual health and progress.

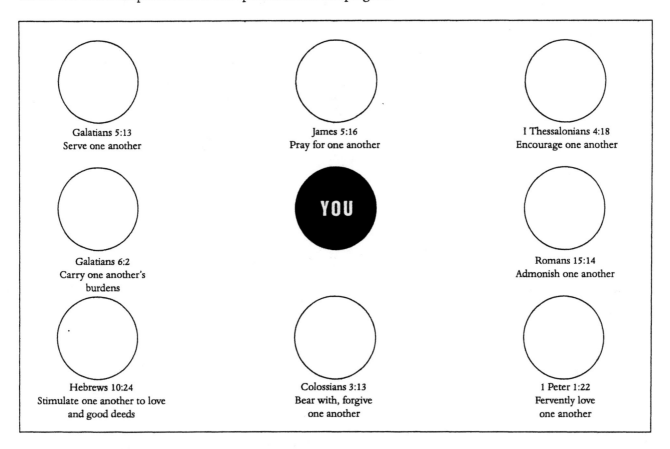

Above are nine circles, and the center one represents you. The other circles symbolize the "one another" relationships essential to your spiritual growth. Read each verse and then draw an arrow between the "you" circle and those circles that represent the kind of "one another" relationship that you have experienced in the last month or so. If you ministered to someone in that way, draw the arrow pointing away from you. If you both received and ministered, make two arrows. Then, in the appropriate circle(s) write the name(s) or initials of the people with whom these relationships occurred.

 Based on this exercise, one strength I see in my relationships is...

Based on this exercise, one weakness I see in my relationships is...

What relational pattern(s) did you notice about yourself in this exercise?

4 What are some advantages of being in close, intimate relationships with other people? Try to list eight. (Hint: Begin with the eight benefits you discovered in the "My Life in Community" exercise.)

Lessons From a Water Basin

On the night before His crucifixion, Jesus met in an Upper Room with His disciples to prepare them to carry on God's work after He was no longer with them (John 13-16). In John 13:1-17, Jesus washed His disciples' feet. This amazing act was more than an ordinance to practice, and more than an example of servanthood and humility. Jesus was also teaching His disciples—then and now—the following three lessons from a water basin about a disciple's spiritual growth.

LESSON #1 SALVATION IS ASSURED (JOHN 13:10) First, Jesus wanted His disciples to remember after He was gone that their salvation was certain. Though the eleven disciples would soon betray Jesus, they were loved and forgiven. "He who has bathed needs only to wash his feet, but is completely clean..." (13:10). At the point of salvation, the believer was given a spiritual cleansing. We are to rest in the certainty that we don't need another salvation bath.

LESSON #2 SPIRITUAL GROWTH IS RECIPROCAL (JOHN 13:14) Jesus wanted His disciples to remember after He was gone that they will need one another. Hear what Jesus said: "If I then, the Lord and the Teacher, washed your feet, you also ought to wash one another's feet" (13:14). Though we believers have taken a salvation bath, our feet still get dirty. (By the following morning, for instance, Peter will deny knowing Jesus three times.) Jesus' disciples need to know that they cannot travel the journey toward Christlikeness alone. It may surprise you, but sanctification requires that we believers assume responsibility for one another's progress. Note the wording of John 13:14:

1. "ought": Jesus issues a command, a marching order. He doesn't merely make a suggestion. Metaphorically, foot washing is a nonnegotiable.
2. "wash": The tense of the verb is continuous and ongoing. Foot washing is not to be a one-time act; rather, it is a way of life.
3. "one another's feet": Foot washing is to be mutual. Jesus' disciples will be God's agents in the sanctification process, helping one another to go the distance.

LESSON #3 BELIEVERS WILL PRIORITIZE RELATIONSHIPS (JOHN 13:15-17). Jesus wanted His disciples to remember after He was gone that they were to challenge one another to go higher and farther on the journey of faith, obedience, and love. Believers will humbly and courageously admit that they need one another and will rely on one another for support and challenge. Jesus' followers will verbalize to one another something like the words written below. Imagine standing with a Christian friend, looking each other in the eyes, and exchanging the following words:

In obedience to Jesus' command, I invite you to be a part of my life and my spiritual growth. I know I can go farther on the journey if we travel together. I am even willing to let you wash my *dirty* feet. I will try to be honest. And I need you to be real with me. Don't overlook any dirt you may see in my life. And I will attempt to support and challenge you in your spiritual growth—whatever the cost or risk.

5 What would you want to say to a fellow believer to invite him/her to join you on the journey? What vow of support and accountability would you like a fellow believer to make to you? Personalize the preceding statement, writing your own words of commitment. Keep in mind that these are words of commitment that you and your friend would say to each other.

Obstacles to Community

We really do need one another! As we've begun to see in the teachings of the New Testament, godly relationships are a greenhouse for our growth from Child to Young Adult to Parent, for our journey toward Christlikeness and spiritual maturity. As you may have already experienced, interpersonal relationships are key to your spiritual growth.

Despite the importance of Christian community, the Bible's teachings on community and relationships are too often given inadequate attention these days. That lack of attention slows down the development and spiritual growth of the Child, Young Adult, and Parent in the faith. We believers must recover an understanding of a distinctively Christian community—a biblical *koinonia*—and make our involvement in that community a priority. Community is not optional; it is not an elective.

 Besides inadequate teaching, what other obstacles to *koinonia* community exist in today's society?

Pilgrims in Progress

Many believers find the type of relationships described in "My Life in Community" and "Prioritize Relationships" quite foreign to their experience. One reason is that community doesn't just automatically happen. Building community must be a high priority and a goal toward which we work. Healthy relationships will not happen without commitment, effort, and "one another" skills.

Readiness for the Milestone #3

Milestone #3 is similar to Milestone #1 and Milestone #2 in that relational maturity—like having both a clear identity grounded in God's grace (Milestone #1) and an accurate concept of God (Milestone #2)—is beyond the capabilities of adolescents. Studies in the process of socialization indicate that, over the course of a lifetime, we progress from dependence on others to independence and then to interdependence. Adolescent interactions are typically shaped by the desire for social acceptance and conformity to established peer expectations. Acutely aware of behavior that earns them approval, adolescents emulate others. Adolescents also tend to still be too concerned about establishing their own identity to be able to establish truly intimate relationships with others. Keep these developmental truths in mind as you consider your spiritual growth.

At whatever age you became a Christian, the Childhood stage of faith started at that point and, ideally, work on Milestones #1, #2 and #3 would have begun. But however long ago you became a Christian, you may not yet be experiencing *koinonia* or mutual care-giving. Relationships characterized by mutual support and challenge even elude many adults. Know that, in order to enjoy an authentic and mature Christian faith, you will need to make sure that you have done the work of Milestone #3.

Your Guide: The Mentoring Parent

At each step of your spiritual journey, you will benefit from the insight and experience of one who has already traveled before you. Such a Parent in the faith would have worked through the tasks of Milestone #3 and will be experiencing rich relationships with fellow believers where he/she finds mutual support and challenge for the journey of faith. As part of a community characterized by New Testament *koinonia*, the Parent in the faith is qualified to share his/her personal story and guide you on your spiritual journey. A Young Adult in the Faith can also serve as a valuable role model.

What skills might a Parent in the faith need to instruct and encourage the believer working on the tasks of Milestone #3?

Warning!

In this lesson we've seen how God's reprogramming grace may come to us through our relationships with His people. But too often these healthy relationships are absent from our lives.

 Study the two scenarios below. Which one, if either, reflects your experience? If the first reminds you of yourself, what will you do to find a caring and wise Parent? If you see yourself in the second scenario, what steps toward finding healthy support from God's people will you take this week?

Scenario #1:

When we believers do not receive adequate care-giving from fellow believers, we are not likely to progress far on our journey toward Christlikeness. Children in the Faith benefit from a biblical map of growth stages (1 John 2:12-14) as well as a wise veteran guide to help them move ahead.

Scenario #2:

Sometimes believers are cloned after the likeness of a leader or discipler who disregards an individual's stage of faith and unique needs. Excessive attachment to such a person can be abusive. Children in the faith may find their beliefs and behaviors rigidly predetermined; they may be trained to jump through prescribed hoops and spiritual disciplines rather than to find their own identity in Christ.

A Closing Prayer

Father in heaven, give me the courage to risk being open and vulnerable... the courage to accept other people's love... and the grace to extend that love to others.... May I see people through Your eyes and find myself increasingly able to love them as You would have me love them.... And when people in my community of believers love me, may I experience it as an extension of Your love.... I pray in Jesus' name. Amen.

Lesson 6

Milestone #3 Growing Up Together
Part 2

The Childhood Stage:
The Birth of Faith

Milestone #1

Experiencing Grace and Forgiveness
To grow spiritually, I need to believe that I am loved unconditionally. Once I am certain of God's forgiveness and confident that He accepts me in Christ, I will be able to discard pretense and my masks and receive His healing.

Milestone #2

Embracing God as Father
To grow spiritually, I need to know God as my Father, as the One in whom I can trust and to whom I can surrender my life. In order to know God as Father, I will replace my distorted ideas of God with biblical truth about Him and then let my heavenly Father re-parent me.

Milestone #3

Growing Up Together
To grow spiritually, I need to experience the mutually supportive and challenging relationships that can be found in the family of God. After all, we who are God's children grow whole when we're in community, not in isolation. We really do need one another.

God calls those of us who name His Son "Lord" into fellowship with one another, a fellowship that is to be light in this dark world and a means of spiritual health and growth for us. But exactly why is Christian fellowship so important? And what are the obstacles to such fellowship? This lesson addresses those issues and closes with a review of the three milestones of Childhood before you move on to the milestones of Young Adulthood.

Aims of Lesson #6

Plan to spend about two hours completing this lesson and preparing for your small-group time. During your time of personal study, you will:

♦ Look at obstacles to experiencing the support and challenge of *koinonia* with fellow believers
♦ Consider skills essential to building community
♦ Continue to develop a biblical understanding of community

In the second part of this lesson, you will:

♦ Review the Childhood stage of faith
♦ Evaluate the three milestones of Childhood
♦ Answer the question, "In what specific ways am I still a child in the faith?"

For Small-Group Leaders:

We recommend that during the ninety-minute study portion of this meeting, group members discuss the following questions.

Lesson 6
1, 2-3 (men), 4 (women), 5, 7

You will not be able to give equal time to each question. So, as the group leader, budget your time carefully.

Retracing Our Steps

God takes us, receives us, and loves us just the way we are—but He will not leave us that way! As God's son or daughter, you are in for a complete overhaul, and that transformation takes place in the body of Christ where you can experience the love and support of brothers and sisters in the Lord. Spiritual growth and healing happen in such relationships. And, as a fellow believer notes, "There are companions along the way as well. One pilgrim may help another as when a blind man carries upon his back one who is lame, so that together they may make a pilgrimage that neither could make alone."

Overview of Milestone #3
Growing Up Together

Milestone #3, "Growing Up Together," focuses on God's grace and how we can be experience it—by both extending it and receiving it—within a community of His people. In the context of healthy interdependent relationships, we come to know God's grace more fully. We also learn to be open about ourselves with others; to perceive life and reality more accurately; and to receive support and encouragement for the slow and sometimes painful process of becoming more like Christ. The tasks of Milestone #3 challenge you to find among God's people a home, a place to belong, and the synergy of mutual care.

In relationships characterized by grace, God's love and forgiveness come alive. The truths set forth in Milestone #1 and #2— the truths that you are forgiven by God and that we can surrender our will and our very life to Him—are "caught" and more fully realized in the context of Christian relationships. Similarly, any unfinished work left over from Milestone #1 and Milestone #2 will manifest itself in your relationships (if not now, then later), and being able to identify those weak places helps you—and all of us!—grow rather than stay stuck.

Remember that in the formative and therefore vulnerable Childhood stage of faith, we are being readied to experience the firsthand faith of the Young Adult. Believers first need a relationally rich environment so that they will gradually own their inner convictions about matters of faith.

Based on the apostle John's statements: "I am writing to you, little children [*teknia*]" in 1 John 2:12, "brethren" (3:14), "one another" (3:11), and "beloved" (4:7)—Milestone #3 offers you a new awareness of the importance of relationships. This new perspective is based on the fact that we are all *teknia* whether we are in the Childhood, Young Adulthood, or Parenthood stage of faith. In Milestone #3, then, we focus on developing mutually supportive and challenging relationships in which we are committed to one another's spiritual growth and wholeness.

Moving Away From... In Milestone #3, you will work on moving away from superficial, detached, impoverished, and unhealthy relationships. You will work on moving away from relationships of proximity, relationships that lack real community. (In Western cultures such unhealthy relationships are often characterized by self-sufficiency and anonymity. People in Eastern cultures, however, are often overly dependent on family and friends, and that can also lead to unhealthy relationships.)

Moving Toward... As you move away from unhealthy relationships, you will be moving toward relationships characterized by an empowering mix of support and challenge. You'll experience "group grace"; a sense of truly belonging; collaborative care; interdependence; and efforts to ensure each person's wholeness in Christ. A special place exists for mentoring Parents in such a matrix of relationships.

Roadblocks to Relationships

Choose two of the following seven options to complete the following sentence. Be ready to share your ideas in the group. You can expect an interesting discussion as you candidly explain your choices and carefully listen to the perspectives and experiences that others share.

 "In my estimation, these are the main stumbling blocks to experiencing genuine Christian community:"

1. We don't know one another's needs.

2. We don't want to know one another's needs.

3. We don't want others to know our needs.

4. We don't take time to know one another deeply.

5. We don't get to know one another deeply in the time we spend together.

6. We don't need one another.

7. We don't know that we need one another.

In what ways might a small group or special Christian friend help us experience genuine Christian community?

For Men Only!

Many men in the West have been conditioned and essentially programmed to be independent, invincible, self-sufficient, and competent. Men are often characterized as competitive, too rational, unemotional, afraid of being vulnerable, and ruggedly individualistic.

 Why might this male image affect the way some male Christians relate to fellow believers?

In what ways might this male mind-set impact the way some male Christians relate to Christ?

The modern male has been described as "the cardboard Goliath." It's also been said that, "the blueprint for masculinity is a blueprint for self-destruction." [1]

 Describe the points at which God's blueprint for spiritual growth and relationships runs counter to the culture's message to men about how they should act. Consider, for instance, Scripture verses from "My Life in Community" (page 39) and "Prioritize Relationships" (page 40).

For Women Only!

 Complete the following sentence according to your perspective and experience. "Many women have been conditioned and even programmed to be..."

Why might this female image affect the way some female Christians relate to fellow believers?

In what ways might this female mind-set impact the way some female Christians relate to Christ?

Describe the points at which God's blueprint for spiritual growth and relationships runs counter to the culture's message to women about how they should act. Consider, for instance, Scripture verses from "My Life in Community" (page 39) and "Prioritize Relationships (page 40)."

Renewed in Relationship

What kinds of relationships are necessary for your spiritual growth? The New Testament is emphatic about what characterizes those relationships that help move us toward Christlikeness. Follow along in your Bible the progression of ideas in Romans 12:1-21, and you'll see that spiritual growth cannot be a private undertaking.

An Imperative: Be Transformed!

Romans 12:1-2 You are transformed as you present yourself to God as a living sacrifice. Conformity to the world will slow your spiritual growth.

Spiritual Gifts That Transform

Romans 12:3-8 Other believers join us at the altar when we present ourselves as a living sacrifice to God. The exercise of spiritual gifts among believers helps us to be transformed and counter conformity to the world.

Relationships That Transform

Romans 12:9-21 Paul notes which kinds of relationships need to exist so that spiritual gifts can function and, in turn, the believer's transformation can occur. When these behaviors are absent, personal spiritual growth is detained, and spiritual gifts become quite unnecessary.

 Why can superficial, unhealthy, or impoverished relationships delay an individual's spiritual growth? In what ways can such relationships affect the exercise of one's spiritual gifts?

Look closely at Romans 12:9-21. What skills or behaviors for building Christian community are mentioned in this passage? Which one might be especially helpful right now in your efforts to strengthen your relationships either within your small group or outside of it? Explain.

A Review of the Childhood Stage of Faith

Each of the three milestones is a powerful catalyst for healthy change and spiritual growth. As we have seen, the Childhood stage of faith is not child's play, a remedial course, or an elective class. Every Christian must master the truths of Childhood. No exceptions, prodigies, or spiritual superkids can rush through or skip any of the three milestones.

As for chronological age, don't be fooled by adults who have plateaued in the Childhood stage of faith, regardless of how long they have been believers. They can't help but see themselves, God, and others from the perspective of that stage. One more caveat about age: neither children nor adolescents are capable of fully engaging or mastering these milestones.

Far too often these three milestones are neglected and the work done on them inadequate! That fact explains why many of us have been Christians for years but have not found the healing and joy we so badly need and want.

According to John's model of spiritual growth, during the Childhood stage of faith, we work on:

◆ Getting firmly in place both the *internal* structure of our identity and our concept of God (Milestones #1 and #2) and the *external* structure of our relationships with other people (Milestone #3).

◆ Receiving divine healing. We cannot blame our culture, our parents, or our earlier experiences for who we are today. Each of us is responsible for who we are and what we do in the present. We are not helpless victims of the past— and we are not to regard ourselves as such! But at the same time we dare not ignore the past. Our understanding of self, God, and others is unconsciously shaped and misshaped in our early years. So the pain we feel as adults, the consequences of dysfunctions in our past, hurts we haven't forgiven, unhealthy habits we've developed, and hungerings we haven't silenced cannot and should not be ignored or denied. Rather, they become the very agenda items that the milestones of Childhood address. Furthermore, Parents in the faith will make rich use of the stuff of our past as they offer us care, guidance, and God's love and point us to the hope we have in Him.

◆ Realizing that being precedes *doing*. Who we are determines what we do. Our actions are predicated on our identity. True spirituality is rooted in being, not doing.

◆ Moving from pretense to authenticity. As you attend to these Childhood milestones, you will discover yourself becoming increasingly genuine, free, and whole. You will experience a renewal of faith and unexpected joy.

We work on these aspects of the Childhood milestones throughout our life, strengthening our concept of self and enriching both our concept of God and our relationships with others as we go along. The guardrails we build as we do so enable us to travel far on our journey of faith even when the path is treacherously rocky and steep.

A Stage of Vulnerability

The original Greek makes it clear that, in 1 John 2:18-27, the apostle seemed to particularly address those believers who have work yet to do in the Childhood stage of faith. Verse 18 begins, "Children [*paidia*], it is the last hour." John then closed this paragraph with "These things I have written to you [*paidia*] concerning those who are trying to deceive you" (verse 26). *Paidia* is the Greek word for the young child who needs guidance, protection, and instruction. This description best fits believers in the Childhood stage. John emphasized that, in this foundational stage, the believer is particularly and uniquely vulnerable to the deception, lies, and counterfeits which the world, the flesh, and the devil (2:15-17) use in their attempts to stall our spiritual progress. Further evidence that 1 John 2:18-27 targets those in the Childhood stage of faith is found in the fact that those in the Young Adulthood stage have already overcome the Evil One (Milestone #6).

The apostle also reminded the vulnerable Children in the faith that they have the Holy Spirit, the Resident Tutor, within them (2:20, 27). His job is to help them recognize false teachers and courageously defeat the three enemies to spiritual growth (verse 27). In addition, John wanted them to know that, living in the "last hour," they must learn to rely on the authority of God's Word as the map for their spiritual journey, rather than depending on teachers and the influences of the group. But this relocation of authority—coming to rely on ourselves to understand Scripture—is still beyond the experience of these believers.

Children Without Childhood

It may surprise you to realize that the pace of spiritual growth can be too slow as well as too fast. First, growth may be too slow and sometimes stop altogether. You may have heard it said that childhood is magic but prolonged infancy is tragic! It's okay and even necessary to be a child for a while, but too many adults remain stuck in the Childhood stage, some permanently plateauing there.

In addition to happening too slowly, spiritual growth can also be pushed to happen too quickly. But healthy and genuine growth cannot be pressured or unduly accelerated. Furthermore, we should never deny the believers their Childhood in the faith. We should not try to hurry the process of spiritual growth or expect too much too soon. Pushing believers into spiritual Young Adulthood or Parenthood will mean incomplete spiritual development in the Childhood stage.

 What happens when children are coddled and allowed to stay babies?

What happens when children are pushed to grow up too quickly?

What do your real-life observations about physical growth and development suggest about what happens in one's spiritual development when the pace is unnaturally too slow or too fast?

The Three Milestones of the Childhood Stage of Faith

As we've seen, John described three characteristics of the Childhood stage of faith. Based on these traits, the three milestones of Childhood address fundamental and far-reaching core issues that, once in place, will guide you toward spiritual maturity. None of the three milestones can be neglected without negatively affecting your spiritual health and delaying, if not preventing, your spiritual growth. All three need to crystallize. Some of us may even need a competent professional counselor to help us work through any underlying issues that paralyze our attempts to establish a healthy identity based on truths in God's Word, a biblical concept of God, and intimate relationships with other people. These three milestones form the foundation for future spiritual growth and determine the quality of our journey toward Christlikeness. The matters addressed in these milestones are basic to the promised joy (1:4) that too often eludes us.

If you don't attend to the three milestones of Childhood, you will have a difficult time later. Unfinished business in the Childhood stage means spiritual dysfunction today and tomorrow. It can't be overemphasized that your future spiritual growth depends on the quality of work you do on the tasks of Milestones #1, #2 and #3. Being renewed by these milestone truths is a precondition to your successful transition into the Young Adulthood stage of faith.

Milestone #1— Experiencing God's Grace and Forgiveness

Your spiritual growth will be sustained by the assurance that you are loved and fully forgiven by God. Your self-worth, your security in who God created you to be, and your sense of significance as a person must be grounded in God's certain, unconditional, and nonrepayable grace. Furthermore, this grace is the basis for spiritual renewal and all growth toward Christlikeness.

When we do not attend to this milestone, our spiritual growth will be blocked, if not completely, at least in those areas where we need healing. An attitude of self-condemnation, our attempts to earn acceptance based on our performance, and an inadequate self-esteem can easily take hold. Our failure to embrace God's grace not only suggests an inadequate view of God (Milestone #2) but it also can prevent deeper relationships in a community (Milestone #3).

Milestone #2 — Embracing God as Father

A person's first idea of God is caught in early childhood experiences. Interpersonal relationships with parents and other significant authority figures, as well as the unique contributions of life events, all of these shape our impressions of God. Case in point. When we hear God called "Father," we naturally think of our parents and the quality of our relationship with them.

If we do not attend to this milestone, distorted ideas about God persist and can even cripple us on our journey of faith. Realize, too, that since no parent flawlessly models the love, forgiveness, and care of our heavenly Father, all of us need to revise our concept of God. Only when we truly know God as He is—according to the truth of the Bible, not the experiences of our youth—can we fully trust Him and surrender our lives to Him.

Milestone #3 — Growing Up Together

We all know the longing to belong, the desire to matter to others. As children of God, however, we can find a sense of belonging in His family. We are privileged recipients of God's forgiveness and grace, and so we share together in the experience of His acceptance and His affirming love. In this context, empowering and caring relationships with fellow believers can spur us on to Christlikeness. This mutual love found in the community of believers is a distinguishing mark of authentic Christian living, and this mutual love is vital to personal spiritual growth.

If we do not attend to this milestone, we will remain either tragically isolated from, or at the other end of the spectrum, unhealthily fused to the family of brothers and sisters in Christ whose nurturing, and companionship on the journey we so need. These days, however, any recognition of the importance of this horizontal dimension of faith is largely absent from our understanding of how faith develops. Spiritual growth requires that others be present emotionally for us. Superficial, distant relationships are not sufficient for moving the believer toward wholeness and Christlikeness.

Having looked at the three milestones of the Childhood stage of faith, now think about them as functioning much like the ropes that climbers use in rappelling. Made of separate strands braided into a single line, those ropes can hold hundreds of pounds, yet those ropes braided together are only about as thick as a person's index finger. Likewise, these three milestones of Childhood, woven together, form a strong lifeline for your spiritual growth.

An Obstruction to Progress

Something from your past may still be influencing the way you act, feel, and think today. Have you asked God to heal you where you have been hurt... to soften you where you have been hardened... to patch the cracks in your faith... to help you release any baggage from the past? God can and will free you from crippling patterns and the aftermath of painful experiences. He can bring divine healing. Besides identifying where you need God's healing and freeing touch, you can probably now also identify which milestones tasks in the Childhood stage of faith you need to attend to. (If you have completed the "Spiritual Growth Profile," look at the five items for each of the three milestones.)

 In what specific ways are you still in the Childhood stage of faith? Explain.

A Closing Prayer

Take some time now to listen to God. What does He have to say to you about any unfinished business in the Childhood stage of faith that is getting in the way of your relationship with Him and your relationships with others? Are you happy with how your journey towards Christlikeness is going in the Childhood stage? Why or why not? Are you moving ahead as you want to? What might you need to do to move forward? Where do you think He would have you go from here?

 In response to the preceding questions, write down some of your thoughts as a prayer. Let your words become a touchstone for your journey of faith. In the future, you'll be able to look back on what you write here and thank God for where He will have taken you.

Lesson 7

Milestone #4 Owning a Firsthand Faith
Part 1

The Young Adulthood Stage:
The Ownership of Faith

Milestone #4

Owning a Firsthand Faith
To grow spiritually, I need to establish ownership of a distinct, personal faith. Having worked through Milestones #1, #2, and #3, I now have a healthy foundation on which to continue to build my faith. My need to conform will diminish as I rely on biblical principles and values I have examined and internalized as my own.

Milestone #5

Linking Truth and Life

Milestone #6

Defeating the Enemies of Spiritual Progress

As you worked through the three milestones of Childhood, you were laying a solid foundation for your journey of faith. Now you are ready to grow into the Young Adulthood stage of faith.

Here at Milestone #4 you'll address the issues reflected in these questions: "*Why* do you believe and behave as you do?" and "To what degree are your beliefs and values largely determined by the approval of other people?" Your beliefs cannot be dictated by your parents, your pastor, your denominational statement of faith, your peer group, or a faith hero—and truly be yours! To become a strong Christian, you need to clarify and own the biblical values and beliefs that will guide your journey of faith. Strong Christians have done so and have therefore learned to stand alone and confidently in their faith.

We will also discover why too many Christian adults plateau and then remain stuck at Milestone #4.

Aims of Lesson #7

This pivotal lesson, which introduces some important new concepts, runs longer than others in the series, so plan to spend at least two hours completing this lesson and preparing for your small-group time. During your time of personal study, you will:

◆ Note spiritual progress you've made beyond the Childhood stage of faith
◆ Discover in Romans 14-15, the differences between the strong believer and the weak
◆ Explore Westerhoff's four styles of faith and trace your personal story of progress in the faith

For Small-Group Leaders:

We recommend that during the ninety-minute study portion of this meeting, group members discuss the following questions.

**Lesson 7
1-9**

You will not be able to give equal time to each question above. So, as the group leader, budget your time carefully. And be sure to allow a half an hour to share questions 7-9.

☑ Note:

Before reading through this Milestone, take a moment to glance at your **Spiritual Growth Profile**. Looking briefly at that mirror to your spiritual journey will help you put the coming discussion into the more personal context of your own spiritual growth.

The Young Adulthood Stage of Spiritual Growth

So far in our study of spiritual growth based on 1 John, we have looked at the first three milestones that we Christians must attend to when we begin our journey of faith. Having moved through the Childhood stage, we are now traveling on to the Young Adulthood stage of faith.

Remember that the stages of this journey are sequential (we pass through them in the same order) and cumulative (they build on one another as we progress). All of us will address the same milestone issues along the way, but we won't travel in the same way or at the same speed. Each of us has our own timetable. Just as no two people are alike, no two journeys towards wholeness and Christlikeness will be identical.

These are the milestones of the Young Adulthood stage of faith:

Milestone #4 — Owning a Firsthand Faith (two lessons)
Milestone #5 — Linking Truth and Life
Milestone #6 — Defeating the Enemies of Spiritual Progress

In 1 John 2:12-14, the apostle John used the Greek word for "young men" to refer to those people in the prime of life, to individuals at the peak of their strength and development. [1] Therefore our use of "young adult" in this study is not to be confused with youthful adolescence. Also, "young men" is changed to Young Adult so as to easily include both genders.

During our spiritual Young Adulthood, we will determine our own sense of ultimate purpose and meaning and decide what is really important to us. Basic personal values, convictions, and commitments are shaped and prized in this stage, and the key word here is *ownership*. We must own our Christian faith rather than believe merely because someone else believes. So during this Young Adult stage you will do the hard work necessary to personalize and experience a faith that is truly your own.

As you transition from spiritual Childhood into Young Adulthood, you can expect to find:

◆ **A New Agenda**
Each of the three milestones is a powerful catalyst for change and growth. As you attend to the tasks of each new milestone, God will move you closer toward Christlikeness and spiritual maturity. During this stage, you will develop additional skills for use on your faith journey.

◆ **A New Perspective**
During the Young Adulthood stage of faith, you will come to see God, self, and others differently than you did when you were in the Childhood stage of faith. You will gain a deeper and increasingly mature Christian perspective on life, faith, and joy (1:4). You'll experience greater freedom and gain a clearer sense of what is real. To your surprise, you may also discover that the believer in the Childhood stage may be threatened by people like you who are farther along on the journey of Christian faith.

◆ **New Challenges**
One challenge of spiritual Young Adulthood comes as you attend to the tasks of Milestones #4, #5, and #6 and recognize the existence of unfinished business left over from the Childhood stage of faith. In addition, the Young Adulthood stage challenges you to learn to stand alone and confident in your biblical convictions. The danger lies in not examining and revising your faith and instead simply conforming and believing what others believe. When we chose that option our faith remains secondhand and borrowed.

◆ **A New Invitation**
Young Adults in the faith are developing a faith that is owned and firsthand. The challenge is to base one's faith on personal convictions rather than merely going along with "acceptable" group-think. Too many Christians plateau here, and stop growing. Choosing to go higher and farther than these believers is worth the risks.

Readiness for the Young Adulthood Stage of Faith

While chronological age is a clue to faith's progress, it is no guarantee of the distance one has traveled because, as we've seen, spiritual growth is never automatic. The Young Adulthood stage of faith can begin as early as age seventeen or eighteen. Deep principled reasoning and ownership of examined beliefs and values are beyond the capabilities of the younger adolescent. [2]

Readiness for a full expression of the stage of Young Adulthood that is both consistent and coherent is not likely before age thirty. It's also important to note that many believers remain stalled in this stage of spiritual development. [3] For some adults, the transition to the Young Adulthood stage of faith can be a protracted process that takes place in the thirties and forties. As you review the Young Adult milestones in these next four lessons, you will begin to understand why.

Overview of Milestone #4: Owning a Firsthand Faith

In Milestone #3, we focused on community, the horizontal dimension of our Christian faith. We acknowledged our need to belong and the importance of mutually supporting and challenging one another to grow in our walk of faith. Milestone #3 emphasized interdependence and bonding attachment to fellow believers. Now, in Milestone #4, a key task is separation, and these two—separation and attachment—will remain in dynamic tension throughout our journey toward Christlikeness. After all, the purpose of community is neither conformity (we believe and behave alike) nor obsessive reliance on others (we let others think for us). In healthy relationships, we are liberated to come into our own internalized biblical faith.

Based on 1 John 2:14 ("I have written to you, young men, because you are strong"), Milestone #4 addresses the core issue of becoming a Christian of distinction, of living your life according to your choices rather than bowing unthinkingly to the pressure to conform to other believers. The truth to live out here is: "I am determining and owning the Christian values and biblical beliefs that, regardless of the cost, will guide my faith journey."

Moving Away From... In Milestone #4 you will work on moving away from secondhand, borrowed faith and external conventions—from obsessive conformity and compliance; from the need to win approval; from being overly concerned about disappointing others; from "pew pressure" to live according to prescribed or stereotypical rules, standards, and expectations; from "fictional sins"; from an unexamined faith and values; and from dependency and imitation.

Moving Toward... As you move away from secondhand faith in Milestone #4, you will work on moving toward firsthand, owned faith and inner convictions—toward a consistent and coherent Christian faith; examined and revised but still biblical values; a faith governed by internalized and inviolable Christian principles; and tolerance of nonessential differences between you and fellow believers.

The Strong Christian: A Profile

Owning one's faith makes one strong in that faith. What steps can we take to become "strong" Christians? What exactly makes a Christian "strong"? We'll begin to answer those questions by stating first that strong believers and weak believers are fundamentally different from one another. As we read in Romans 14 and 15, the weak Christian is one whose beliefs and values are "borrowed" and often dependent upon the approval of significant others. A weak Christian's faith is largely unexamined and secondhand. (Think of the Jewish Christians clinging on to hundreds of years of inherited traditions.) The danger of such a secondhand faith is "a reliance on significant others to such an extent that personally held beliefs and values are never consciously adopted or reflected upon. What arises is a truncated value system in which one simply 'buys into' the values of others in his or her life who are admired." [4]

In contrast, strong Christians are moving away from secondhand faith and conventions–from being motivated by prescribed rules, controlling standards, "oughts," "shoulds," and the need for approval. Strong Christians are moving toward firsthand faith and internalized convictions–toward a life governed by self-chosen biblical principles. As we discuss this growth, we will discover why many Christians fail to make this risky transition to the Young Adulthood stage of faith.

The Weak and the Strong

In a change of pace and format in this study, read Romans 14:1-12 below. You may be surprised by how relevant these verses are to a Young Adult in the faith.

1 Now accept the one who is weak in faith, but not for the purpose of passing judgment on his [the weak] opinions. 2 One person [the strong] has faith that he may eat all things, but he who is weak eats vegetables only. 3 The one who eats [the strong] is not to regard with contempt the one who does not eat [the weak], and the one who does not eat is not to judge the one who eats, for God has accepted him [the strong]. 4 Who are you [the weak] to judge the servant of another? To his own master he [the strong] stands or falls; and he will stand, for the Lord is able to make him stand. 5 One person regards one day above another, another regards every day alike. Each person [strong and weak] must be fully convinced in his own mind. 6 He who observes the day, observes it for the Lord, and he who eats, does so for the Lord, for he gives thanks to God; and he who eats not, for the Lord he does not eat, and gives thanks to God.

7 For not one of us [strong or weak] lives for himself, and not one dies for himself; 8 for if we live, we live for the Lord, or if we die, we die for the Lord; therefore whether we live or die, we are the Lord's. 9 For to this end Christ died and lived again, that He might be Lord both of the dead and of the living. 10 But you [strong], why do you judge your brother [weak]? Or you again [the strong], why do you regard your brother [the weak] with contempt? For we shall all [strong and weak] stand before the judgment seat of God. 11 For it is written, "As I live, says the LORD, every [strong and weak] knee shall bow to Me, and every tongue [strong and weak] shall give praise to God." 12 So then each one of us [strong and weak] will give an account of himself to God.

Now read through the following observations about the Romans 14 passage you just read. As you do so, know that you are laying an important foundation for the Young Adulthood and Parenthood stages of growth.

Conformity & Secondhand Faith: Coming to a Crossroads

The early church in Rome consisted primarily of Gentile Christians; Jewish Christians were in the minority. But both groups had to deal with an important question about conformity: Would the Jewish Christians continue to conform to their deeply rooted historical traditions and practices? According to Paul, the Gentile Christians did not need to conform to those Jewish ways—but what would that mean for the fellowship? At stake in the church at Rome was much more than food taboos and which feast days to observe. Church unity was threatened. [5]

Born a Jew himself, Paul understood that Jewish Christians were alarmed by the idea of abandoning the very traditions that had given them their identity as God's chosen people. Laws governing diet and the observance of the Sabbath were among the clearest boundary markers that set Jews apart from Gentiles. The Sabbath had become a badge of ethnic identity and devotion to ancestral custom. Paul, however, was also concerned about the harsh insensitivity of Gentile Christians who didn't understand the Jewish customs and the value the Jews placed on them. [6] These stronger "liberal" believers regarded the scruples of the traditionalist Jews as tolerable but worthy of contempt, and the weaker "conservative" Jewish believers—fewer in number and lower in social and political standing—regarded the freer practice of the liberal Gentiles as completely intolerable. As Christianity, an essentially Jewish movement, began to develop its own distinctive character and identity, it had to confront these very sensitive issues. The issue was earliest Christianity's understanding of itself. Conformity for conformity's sake was not the answer for either the Jewish believers or the Gentile believers, all of whom who had a personal relationship with Jesus.

It was to this community that Paul addressed the question, "What should be the church's response to the minority opinion of the weaker Jewish believers?" Put differently, what should be the church's response to questions about conformity? Just as the early church found itself at a crossroads, every growing believer does as well. Will you choose to conform to the faith you've grown up with, the faith you've settled comfortably into, the faith that you've borrowed or adopted and that may be too dependent on the approval of other people—or will you choose the other option and take the step of examining your Christian values, identifying essential and nonessential differences between believers, and making your convictions about your faith your own? Choosing the latter can result in a personal crisis of introspection and wrestling with key issues—but know that the effort is worth it.

Dismantling Conformity & Moving beyond Secondhand Faith

The "weak in faith" (Romans 14:1) were definitely Christians, but their trust in God was clouded by their Jewish heritage and their cautious, scrupulous abstinence from certain activities that had been forbidden them. As one commentator observes, these Jewish Christians were "weak in their faith, but strong in scruples." [7] They put too much weight on the outward form as the covenant people and on their status as the chosen people of Israel (Romans 2:17-29). They were not living out of complete dependence on God as their father Abraham did (Romans 4:19-21). Simply conforming to religious tradition and community values seemed sufficient to them.

So Paul wrote to the strong Gentile believers, "Accept the one who is weak in faith, but not for the purpose of passing judgment on his opinions" (Romans 14:1) and "The one who eats is not to regard with contempt the one who does not eat" (verse 3). There was no room for judging and condemning the weak about their observance of special days and diets. Paul instructed the strong that they should not seek to impose their views and practices on the weak, nor laugh at or despise the weak as narrow-minded. Paul knew that the strong infuriated the weak who considered eating meat an immoral rather than an amoral issue. Rather than attempting to avoid a schism by trying to persuade the weak that their scruples were baseless, Paul encouraged the weak to let God continue to do His work in the hearts of Gentile believers (verse 4).

Let me summarize Paul's message to the strong,

> Your ongoing support and challenge will be a part of the growth and transformation of the weak. Show them how you came to an owned and firsthand faith. Don't be angry at the weak over their beliefs, ungrounded as they are to you, and don't be impatient with them. And you who are strong cannot claim freedom for yourself without allowing freedom to the other.

It is important to note that, as Paul pointed out, the controversy is over mere "opinions" (Romans 14:1), and non-essentials, not matters addressed in Scripture as sin. Believers will inevitably have different opinions on various issues. The Christian community should be able to allow members the freedom, within the limits of biblical Christianity, to embrace divergent views and opinions. The Christian community should not find it necessary to achieve a common mind on every point of possible disagreement.

1 The gospel calls for faith in Jesus, not faith *plus* special days and special practices and not faith *less* certain activities. Making a list of either things to do in addition to believe or of things to refrain from if you believe results in a false definition of Christlikeness, a psuedo-transformation—and the same happens today. What nonessentials of the faith are points of disagreement in the church today?

A Catalyst to Firsthand Faith: Strong Community

Paul knew that the weak in the church at Rome wanted to make their views binding for all believers; they wanted to standardize or codify beliefs and behaviors in order to guarantee uniformity. But Paul told the weak not to "judge" the strong. The weak are not to accuse—either publicly or privately—the strong believers among them of compromise, spiritual indifference, or lack of discipline (14:3-4). Neither are the weak—given to acting as if they are superior to the strong—to criticize and condemn the strong as unscrupulous and irreverent. Nor are the weak advised to simply comply and imitate the strong. Instead, the weak are to accept the strong into the family of believers just as God Himself has.

The Christian community is to function like a greenhouse and optimize the growth of the individual members. The freedom that results from accepting people despite different opinions and behaviors is vital to healthy spiritual growth. The strong and the weak are to accept and welcome one another into community (14:19). But this acceptance cannot be conditional, even when substantial differences of opinion exist, and there is not to be any forced conformity in the Christian community.

2 Think about your own experience with other believers. When, if ever, have you ever felt compelled to conform? When have you felt pressure to believe or behave in a way acceptable to the group? Be specific about the issues involved, the circumstances, your decision, and your feelings at the time.

Another Catalyst to Firsthand Faith: The Lordship of Christ

Many Christians choose to look to other people in the church to determine their beliefs and behaviors, and that tendency results in a secondhand and borrowed faith rather than a vibrant, personal, firsthand, and owned faith. Paul knew human nature, and he knew the difference between doing something out of a sense of *convention* and doing something out of a sense of personal *conviction*. He therefore urged strong and the weak Christians alike to be "fully convinced in [their] own mind" about their faith and their actions as believers (Romans 14:5, 14). Strong Christians are governed by the authority of Christ, not the authority of people who matter to them. Paul continued, "The faith which you have, have as your own conviction before God" (14:22).

What can believers do to move away from a borrowed, secondhand faith? An answer lies in Romans 14 where nine times in verses 4-11 Paul referred to Jesus as "Lord." We Christians are to determine our personal convictions based on the ultimate approval of the Lord because, after all, "We are the Lord's" (verse 8). With this statement, Paul took both the strong and the weak believers back to the fundamental issue of a personal relationship with the Lord. Controversial issues are not to be settled by relying on other people's opinions or conforming to group pressure. God is the ultimate judge and audience. All beliefs and values are to be determined by "What does the Lord think?" rather than "What do others think? Will my course disappoint others?"

 Why can allowing Christ to be Lord help a believer move away from conformity and secondhand faith?

Paul asked several key questions of the Roman congregation–and those questions are just as relevant for us today. Let these questions help you step back and look at your faith and your life. What motivates you to do what you do? Do you tend to rely on other Christians to do your thinking about spiritual issues for you? Do you conform to the expectations of others who matter? Or do you play it safe and merely imitate other believers? Or, conversely, do you choose to be different from the majority simply to be different? What are you doing to determine your own convictions?

 What do your answers to this series of questions show you about how far you have traveled on your journey toward a firsthand faith?

The Whims of the Weak

Are strong believers to accommodate their behavior to the wishes of the weak and thereby be shackled? Are the strong to avoid conflicts at all costs and ask about their every action, "What will others think?" Paul was aware that the weak can manipulate the strong and suffocate the liberty available to them in Christ. One commentator explained it this way: "It often happens that in his very weakness he has an effective weapon for making the circumstances comply with his view. Not infrequently it is the weak who is the real tyrant. In his judgment of others he finds a compensation for his weakness." [8]

To summarize, Paul's words aimed at the weak were blunt, direct and overdue:

> Grow up! Focus on the essentials of faith, not non-essentials. Stop being so defensive and easily offended. As you examine and revise your beliefs and behaviors, and as you transfer your allegiance to the Lord and His Word (rather than the group), know that you are loved and valued in the Body of Christ.

Writing to strong believers as well as weak, Paul said, "Let us not judge one another anymore, but rather determine this—not to put an obstacle or a stumbling block in a brother's way" (verse 13). While all of us who name Jesus as Lord need to be considerate of our brothers and sisters and try to see issues from their point of view, Paul was not calling strong Christians to give in to the whims of the weak. Neither was he merely concerned about the strong disappointing or hurting the feelings of the weak. Instead, Paul called believers to resist the temptation to insist on one's rights, and the primacy of one's own convictions.

Responsible love in the Christian community means living with sensitivity to one another and helping fellow believers. Such love seeks to understand the other person's perspective. Paul therefore urged strong and weak believers alike to consider the needs of others rather than insisting on personal rights. Believers are to be open to ideas different from their own. Paul called Christians in Rome and us today to "pursue the things which make for peace and the building up of one another" (verse 19), but this peace is to be achieved not by avoiding friction or keeping quiet about issues.

What statements in this section "Whims of the Weak" can help you become a stronger believer? Explain.

Paul opened Romans 15 with further instructions for the strong: "Now we who are strong ought to bear the weaknesses of those who are without strength and not just please ourselves. Let each of us please his neighbor for his good, to his edification" (verses 1-2). The strong are not to merely wait for the immature to catch up to where they are. The strong are to intentionally reach out and involve themselves with the weaker Christian. Again, Paul was addressing strong believers who "are full of goodness, filled with all knowledge, and able to admonish one another" (verse 14). The ability to admonish one another suggests that more than superficial relationships exist here. Paul called believers then and now to talk to one another in order to resolve differences. As this process enables people to clarify the issues, increase mutual understanding, and communicate unconditional love, it encourages spiritual growth and authentic community.

 The strong and the weak are fundamentally different from one another and we have summarized those differences. Think about where you are at this point of your Christian journey. In what ways are you strong in the faith? On what points are you weak in the faith? Be specific.

Styles of Faith... Becoming Strong in the Faith

The movement toward Christian maturity and ownership of a strong faith is a dynamic and lifelong process. Religious educator John Westerhoff gives us a helpful way to look at this process when he identifies four styles of faith and likens them to the rings of a tree. As a tree grows and matures, it adds rings, but the previously formed rings are still present in the central core of the tree's trunk. Keep that image in mind as you review the four styles of faith outlined next. [9] Also, know that even if you became a Christian as an adult, you will go through each of the four styles.

Experienced Faith: The Experienced Faith of preschoolers and children is an inherited faith, a faith shaped by children's responses to their experiences with Christians they know. Children copy the faith of others as they observe and interact with members of the Christian community. Questions of belief and doctrine are yet to come.

Affiliative Faith: The Affiliative Faith of our teenage years is shaped by a strong desire to belong, and a sense of belonging comes when our values and actions are determined largely by the church's way of understanding faith. Heritage and traditions shape faith. This is largely a "borrowed faith," a secondhand faith. Typically, adults stall here, Westerhoff observes.

Searching Faith: Searching Faith comes in late adolescence and early young adulthood when believers examine and even challenge their assumptions. Every point of faith is up for scrutiny, and a certain amount of doubt and some critical judgment are necessary at this point of spiritual development. It is not always easy to move away from a faith that belongs to the community to a faith that is one's own.

Owned Faith: Owned Faith can come only after Searching Faith, and at this point your faith is central to your very being and your actions. As one wise believer has observed, faith like Job's–genuinely owned faith–cannot be shaken because it is the result of being shaken. This point of owning your faith is the goal of the Young Adulthood stage of faith.

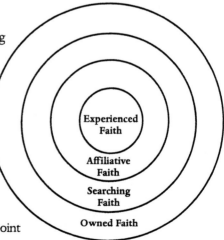

Pilgrims in Progress

Tracing your own growth through these four styles of faith provides you with one way of thinking about your journey of faith.

 7 Do you agree or disagree with Westerhoff's observation that many adults plateau or stall in the Affiliative Style of faith? If you agree, share reasons why the stall might occur here. If you disagree, explain why and offer evidence in support of your position.

 8 What has been your experience of the transition from Affiliative Faith to Searching Faith?

 9 What has been your experience of a Searching Faith? What about it has been challenging? Explain. Know that we probably will not grow strong and come to our own faith without some measure of pain, conflict, or doubts– and these are not necessarily symptoms of sin, a loss of faith, or carnality.

A Closing Prayer

Spend a few quiet moments with your heavenly Father.... Thank Him for your community of believers and ask Him to bless your collective efforts to increase mutual understanding, communicate unconditional love to one another, and encourage the growth of each individual.... Tell God where you are feeling personally challenged about owning your faith—and where you may be feeling afraid to step out on your own convictions... Ask Him to guide you along any new path in your spiritual journey you are wanting to travel... to teach you to live with Jesus as Lord... to rely less on the approval of others... and to give you boldness to internalize and own your faith in Him–regardless of the cost.

Lesson 8

Milestone #4 Owning a Firsthand Faith
Part 2

The Young Adulthood Stage:
The Ownership of Faith

▶

Milestone #4

Owning a Firsthand Faith
To grow spiritually, I need to establish ownership
of a distinct, personal faith. Having worked
through Milestones #1, #2, and #3, I now have
a healthy foundation on which to continue to
build my faith. My need to conform will diminish
as I rely on biblical principles and values I have
examined and internalized as my own.

Milestone #5

Linking Truth and Life

Milestone #6

Defeating the Enemies of
Spiritual Progress

We can define faith as "what a person believes," but that is only the beginning. Faith also includes *why* people believe a certain way and *how* they behave as a result of those beliefs. As you come to own your Christian faith, you will rely on the biblical values you have examined, revised, and internalized and not be as concerned about conforming to the expectations of others. You will be governed by choices you have made carefully and prayerfully.

Sadly, many adults find it all too easy and comfortable to conform, so they stay stuck in their beliefs—bound by prescribed and institutionalized rules, artificial taboos, fictional sins, and an unexamined, secondhand faith. Those of us who choose to examine and come to own our faith may nevertheless live out that faith in a way that closely resembles the way some people live out their secondhand faith. But we will be living that way for different reasons.

Aims of Lesson #8

Don't be surprised if you are tempted to slow down and dwell on certain points in this lesson. I encourage you to take the time to do just that. Milestone #4 is pivotal to your Christian journey. During your time of private study, you will:

◆　Consider the process of coming to own a firsthand faith by examining the third catalyst to growth in Romans 14; three levels in Kohlberg's model of the development of commitment; and two stages in Fowler's faith development theory

◆　Clarify what you can do to move toward the firsthand faith of the strong believer

For Small-Group Leaders:

We recommend that during the ninety-minute study portion of this meeting, group members discuss the following questions.

Lesson 8
1-3, 5-7

You will not be able to give equal time to each question. So, as the group leader, budget your time carefully.

Retracing Our Steps

We can define faith as "what a person believes." A more complete understanding of faith, however, must also include *why* people believe what they do and how those beliefs affect their behavior. A strong Christian is concerned with the why and the how of faith (the process) as well as the what of faith (the content).

Milestone #4 poses such process questions as "Why do you believe and behave as you do?," "Who/what is influencing your values?," and "To which beliefs and actions are you conforming in order to gain people's approval?" Milestone #4 challenges you to become aware of and then confront the unexamined assumptions and prescribed rules that may be weighing you down and even weakening your faith. A word of caution: A well-grounded and lived-out faith, one that is consistent and coherent, is rarely seen in someone younger than thirty. In fact, many adults remain stalled at this stage of spiritual growth and may not be as far along as they think.

 Based on 1 John 2:14 ("I am writing to you, young men, because you are strong"), Milestone #4 addresses the core issue of becoming a Christian of distinction, of living your life according to your choices rather than bowing unthinkingly to the pressure to conform to other believers. The truth to live out here is: "I am determining and owning the Christian values and biblical beliefs that, regardless of the cost, will guide my faith journey."

 **Moving Away From...** In Milestone #4 you will work on moving away from secondhand, borrowed faith and external conventions—from obsessive conformity and compliance; from the need to win approval; from being overly concerned about disappointing others; from "pew pressure" to live according to prescribed or stereotypical rules, standards, and expectations; from fictional sins; from an unexamined faith and values; and from dependency and imitation.

 **Moving Toward...** As you move away from secondhand faith in Milestone #4, you will work on moving toward firsthand, owned faith and inner convictions—toward a consistent and coherent Christian faith; examined and revised but still biblical values; a faith governed by internalized and inviolable Christian principles; and tolerance of nonessential differences between you and fellow believers.

 Often prescribed "oughts" and "shoulds," practices that have become sacred, fictional sins, and artificial taboos keep Christians from growing up in their faith. Identify some of the "oughts," "shoulds," rules, fictional sins, and taboos that you have seen at work in your church experience. Explain why they can slow personal spiritual growth.

What effect did these rules and taboos have on you personally? Be specific.

Moving from Weak to Strong: The Development of Commitment

Too often we believers neglect the process by which we can become strong Christians. If we want to grow strong, we must consider not only our beliefs (are they biblical?) but also how we come to believe what we believe. John Westerhoff offered one model of Styles of Faith, in the preceding lesson. Now we'll consider Lawrence Kohlberg and Catherine Stonehouse's studies of moral maturity to see when and why some believers get stuck. Study the following chart (it's not as complicated as it looks) to learn about the process of becoming morally mature. [1] Then answer the question that follows.

	LEVEL ONE		**LEVEL TWO**		**LEVEL THREE**
Source of Authority	Self-Interest	↑ LIBERATING ELEMENT	External Standards and Models	↑ LIBERATING ELEMENT	Internal Principles
What is Right?	Adult Command	CRISIS POINT — OBEDIENCE	Important People and Groups	CRISIS POINT — TRUST	Self-Chosen Values
Stimulus to Right Action	Reward or Punishment		Perform to Please		Commitment to Inviolable Principles
	COMPLIES		**IDENTIFIES**		**INTERNALIZES**

Level 1: The Preconventional Level (From ages 5 or 6)
At Level 1 of moral maturity, the child's point of reference is himself or herself. At this point of their development, children are egocentric and oblivious to the needs of others. Therefore, their choices are determined by what the consequences of their actions will be, by what reward or punishment they may receive. Children at this point also rely on others to define what is right and wrong. They defer to authorities without question. Sadly, some adults will operate at this exact level of moral reasoning. (Compare Level 1 to John Westerhoff's Experienced Faith, defined in Lesson #7.)

Level 2: The Conventional Level (Teens and early adulthood)
When we are at Level 2 of moral maturity, our reference point is broader than the self. Now we internalize the rules and expectations of family, peer group, and significant others. (We all know, for instance, how intense the need to belong is during adolescence.) The imitation, conformity, compliance, and dependency that result from our awareness of these rules and expectations are largely unconscious. As long as we remain at this level, authority is still external to self, and we are governed by others. Individuals at Level 2 are preoccupied with rules and careful not to disappoint the people and groups they deem important. Again, too many adults operate at this level. (Compare to Westerhoff's Affiliative Faith.)

Level 3: Postconventional Level (Adulthood—but age is no guarantee of arriving at this level)
Teenagers and young adults have not had sufficient time to test their beliefs, but at Level 3 this testing begins. Authority shifts from peer groups and significant others to an "inner panel of experts." Individuals now deliberately search for the reasons behind the rules, and principles become self-chosen (but still biblically based), internal, inviolable, and "mine." Some signs of reaching this level may appear during late adolescence, but it is not until adulthood that this higher form of commitment is firmly established. It is then that the adult can draw on all three levels of moral reasoning. Although a cognitive awareness of principles may develop in adolescence, commitment to their ethical use develops only in adulthood. (Compare to Westerhoff's Searching Faith and Owned Faith.]

∙∙

Note that the weak believers whom Paul talks about in Romans 14:1-12 appear to be at Level 1 or 2 in their moral maturity and the strong appear to be at Level 3.

Catalyst to Firsthand Faith: The Judgment Seat of God

Recall from pages 56-57 that Paul has noted two catalysts to faith that run counter to the forces of conformity and secondhand faith. Paul taught the importance of, first, participating in a strong community and, second, practicing the lordship of Christ. Such participation and practice will indeed help a believer move away from Level 1 or 2 toward Level 3 of moral maturity. In Romans 14:10-12 Paul introduced a third catalyst: the future "judgment seat of God" before which "each one of us [the strong as well as the weak] will give an account of himself to God." Our future judgment should shape our present convictions, and it is this shift of authority—this recognition of God's supreme authority over us which is critical to our becoming a strong believer. Strong Christians realize that they are ultimately accountable to God rather than to the authority and approval of others. The strong live by a higher calling—to please God.

At that future judgment, we will not only be asked whether we named Jesus Christ as our Lord and Savior (the basis of our salvation), but also *how* we were a Christian—*how* our words and actions revealed our commitment to Jesus. In order to effectively live out our faith, each one of us must arrive at our own Christian convictions: Have I consciously chosen to live by these biblical convictions, or do I merely comply with the conventional status quo of my denomination or a certain faith hero? Do my convictions and consequent actions reflect the truth that Jesus is really Lord of my life? To answer these questions, we must carefully examine the beliefs and practices of our faith and be willing to modify them as we make our Christian faith our own. Too many adult believers, however, remain stuck in the Affiliative Faith and do not make the transition to the Searching or the Owned Faith.

 Why can the inevitability of a personal appearance before the judgment seat of God help believers move beyond the conformity of Level 2 to the mature convictions of Level 3?

Moving from Weak to Strong: Lessons from Studies in Faith Development

We've looked at the development of faith from a couple of different angles in order to help us recognize where and why we might be stuck in our spiritual growth. First we saw John Westerhoff's progression from Experienced to Affiliative to Searching and finally to Owned Faith. Then we looked at the three levels of Kohlberg and Stonehouse's study of moral maturity. Now we'll consider a third perspective on faith development, specifically Stages 3 and 4 of James Fowler's model.

Stage 3: Synthetic-Conventional Faith

Prominent in adolescence or early adulthood, Stage 3 faith is secondhand faith largely dependent on conformity. Individuals in this stage are acutely attuned to the approval of others, to the convention of the group, and to external standards—clearly, the center of authority is outside of themselves. During this stage of heroes and the tyranny of the peer group, the ideas, expectations and views of other people are internalized without being examined carefully or objectively. Sadly, the spiritual progress of many adults stops at Stage 3. [2]

Stage 4: Individuative-Reflective Faith

Stage 4 is firsthand faith, and many people begin making the transition to a firsthand faith in late adolescence. A Stage 4 individuative-reflective faith, however, does not become consistently and fully operative until a person's late twenties or early thirties. For some adults, the transition, if it comes at all, may occur in the thirties or forties. By Stage 4, the center of authority has shifted from external to internal—from outer conventions to self-chosen biblical principles and owned convictions. A genuine movement from Stage 3 to Stage 4 means ending one's reliance on external sources of authority. The tyranny of the group must be undermined and authority relocated within the self. The believer now is taking the burden of responsibility for his commitments, lifesyle, and beliefs.

The specific beliefs we choose at this point may be the same ones we grew up with, but our reason for believing them has changed. Old assumptions and values are no longer tacitly held. Our examination of the beliefs we once held may be—and quite often is—accompanied by doubt and questioning, but the effort results in the genuine ownership of one's faith. Not all adults, however, make this transition to Stage 4 faith. Many remain—some permanently—stuck at Stage 3. [3]

 Is it possible that the weak believers Paul talked about in Romans 14 were stuck at Fowler's Stage 3 of faith development? Explain your answer.

 What similarities do you find between Fowler's Stage 4 believers and the strong believers described in Romans 14?

The Strong and the Weak

The following chart summarizes the studies of styles of faith (Westerhoff), moral maturity (Kohlberg) and faith development (Fowler)—three ways of looking at key aspects of the process of spiritual growth. Too often the spiritual growth of believers levels off at a borrowed, secondhand faith—these Christians continue to look to others to determine their beliefs and behaviors, and these weak believers are fundamentally different from strong believers who own their faith.

Romans 14—15	Styles of Faith	Moral Commitment	Faith Development
Weak Believers	Experienced, Affiliative	Level 1—2	Synthetic-Conventional
Strong Believers	Searching, Owned	Level 3	Individuative-Reflective

Note the following four distinctions between the two types of believers.

The weak relate differently to the Word of God.

As Paul's words in Romans 14 indicate, Jewish believers in the Roman church still retained biases deeply rooted in their culture and experiences. How difficult to discard the shackles of—in our terms—an affiliative style of faith (Westerhoff), conventional moral reasoning (Kohlberg), and a synthetic-conventional faith (Fowler), and, as a result, how easy to be stuck in a secondhand faith. God's Word is key to moving us beyond such a secondhand faith. Strong Christians turn to Scripture as they examine their beliefs, and they find the Word of God transforming as it speaks truth that they, by God's Spirit, absorb and apply. Clearly, weak believers do not realize what a powerful agent for growth the living Word of God is.

The values and cherished beliefs of the weak are largely unexamined.

In the Roman church Paul addressed taboos about foods and special days had been become sacred, governing the actions and thoughts of the weak believers. Today, the actions and thoughts of the weak believers are similarly governed by conditioning, conformity, and convention. Strong believers, however, examine their values and beliefs: They systematically reflect on and critically explore the "givens" of their faith (owned faith; individuative-reflective faith). No wonder the Word of God is a more effective agent of transformation in the life of a strong believer.

The weak continue to be governed by convention and external authorities.

In addition to being unexamined, the beliefs of the weak are still largely determined by significant others and by conditioning forces outside of themselves. The weak may have strong convictions, but these believers are not yet released from the bondage of conforming to beliefs held by external authorities. The danger here is that the weak have so completely internalized other people's expectations and evaluations that making their own decisions is quite difficult. In contrast, the strong are governed more by inner conviction and self-chosen biblical principles, and they consider the Lord to be the ultimate authority for their life.

The weak believer's relationships within the Christian community are impoverished.

The weak don't find their beliefs challenged by their community, and even if those beliefs were, the weak wouldn't have the support necessary to examine their beliefs and grow through the process. Spiritual growth happens in an environment where there is a free exchange of ideas and perspectives; exposure to more complex reasoning about one's faith; contact with situations that pose problems, raise questions, and challenge one's current moral structure (the resulting dissatisfaction can help move us to the next level); and the freedom to openly discuss conflicting views.

If the weak suddenly found themselves in such a dynamic environment, these believers—who have complied to the peer pressure of other weak believers and perhaps experienced criticism and rejection from immature Christians—may come to understand the need to examine and own their beliefs. Likewise, in this kind of environment, the strong may gain some insight into the perspectives, feelings, and motivations of the weak.

In writing to the church at Rome, Paul was not simply demanding that the weak comply to his arguments or to the arguments of the strong (with whom he sided). Instead, Paul encouraged the believers—strong and weak alike—to establish relationships with one another characterized by love, edification, and mutual accountability. This kind of accepting and affirming community can foster genuine spiritual growth in the strong and weak alike. This kind of dynamic fellowship can empower individuals to make their own decisions about their faith.

 In what ways does the community of believers in which you are involved compare to the vibrant, healthy spiritual community just described? Be specific.

Pilgrims in Progress

Reflect on what God has been saying to you in this lesson by writing several sentences that begin with the following clause:

 "God seems to have been impressing on me that I... "

 Why might the support of a friend or a small group challenge you and help you move toward owning your faith more fully?

Your Guide: The Mentoring Parent

At each step of your spiritual journey, you will benefit from the insight and experience of someone who has already traveled this road. Such a Parent in the faith would have worked through Milestone #4. As one who owns his/her faith, the Parent is qualified to share his/her personal story and to guide you on your spiritual journey.

 What skills might the Parent in the faith need to empower the Young Adult at Milestone #4?

A Closing Prayer

Almighty God, I confess to You the sense of security I find in long-held beliefs and in fitting in with others... Help me take a step of faith and continue to examine and revise my beliefs, trusting that You will show me Your truth.
May I courageously wrestle with whatever tough questions I encounter—and teach me to live out the faith that is becoming my own... And, God, may I be open to the transforming power of Your Word, the transforming touch of Your grace... I pray in the name of Your Son, my Savior, Jesus Christ. Amen.

Milestone #5 Linking Truth and Life

The Young Adulthood Stage:
The Ownership of Faith

Milestone #4

Owning a Firsthand Faith

To grow spiritually, I need to establish ownership of a distinct, personal faith. Having worked through Milestones #1, #2, and #3, I now have a healthy foundation on which to continue to build my faith. My need to conform will diminish as I rely on biblical principles and values I have examined and internalized as my own.

Milestone #5

Linking Truth and Life

To grow spiritually, I need to allow God's Word to transform me. I will therefore move beyond merely receiving head knowledge from the Bible to, by the power of the Holy Spirit, applying its truth to my life. The Word of God will reside in me and have a centering and guiding influence on me.

Milestone #6

Defeating the Enemies of Spiritual Progress

The Word of God abides in you when you have attended to the previous four Milestones. The Word of God is experienced, not just accepted. The Scriptures will therefore increasingly transform, not just inform you, and they will increasingly define, modify, and order your world.

Moving beyond merely receiving biblical information to experiencing personal transformation, beyond knowing about God's truth to really applying it to real life is what Milestone #5 is all about. Keep in mind that we understand the Bible from our perspective as a Child, a Young Adult, or a Parent in the faith. This lesson, however, talks about moving beyond lower levels of Bible learning to truly incorporating God's truth in our life.

Aims of Lesson #9

Plan to spend two hours completing this lesson and preparing for your small-group time. During your time of personal study, you will:

♦ Consider the Scriptures' ability to go beyond merely informing us to transforming us and making us more like Christ
♦ Examine reasons why we don't apply the Word and experience its power
♦ Discover the interrelationship between the first five milestones of spiritual development

For Small-Group Leaders:

We recommend that during the ninety-minute study portion of this meeting, group members discuss the following questions.

**Lesson 9
1-6**

You will not be able to give equal time to each question above. So, as group leader, budget your time carefully.

☑ Note:

Before reading through this Milestone, take a moment to glance at your **Spiritual Growth Profile**. Looking briefly at that mirror to your spiritual journey will help you put the coming discussion into the more personal context of your own spiritual growth.

Retracing Our Steps

During the Young Adulthood stage of faith, Milestone #4 answers the question, "Why do I believe and behave as I do?" This is vital to moving away from a secondhand, external and unexamined faith toward an owned and firsthand faith.

Overview of Milestone #5
Linking Truth to Life

— "God has not given us His Word only to hear—or even to 'believe'—but primarily to do. We are to get ready for life, not an exam."

— "The Bible is not so much a book as it is a place, *the* place where the soul has its rendezvous with God."

— "Inert ideas about Christian faith lead to inert Christians."

Each of these three statements highlights the truth that knowing *about* God is incomplete without knowing Him personally. Genuine Christian faith is grounded in the Bible and then lived out in the day-to-day world. As you do the work of Milestone #5, you will find yourself experiencing, not merely accepting, the truth and power of God's Word. Your belief and your behavior will merge. You will move beyond simply knowing about Scripture to letting God's Word guide you into a distinctive Christian lifestyle and gradually transform your whole person as well as your life purpose.

Based on 1 John 2:14 ("I am writing to you, young men, because the Word of God abides in you"), Milestone #5 addresses the core issue of centering your life on God's Word. The truth to be learned and integrated into your life is: "The Word is the ultimate authority; its truth is to be internalized and personally applied."

Moving Away From... In Milestone #5, you are working on moving away from abstract biblical information that doesn't result in transformation—from theology that has no impact on biography; from creedal and cerebral faith (the cognitive curse); from reflection without action; and from truth that is accepted but not life-changing.

Moving Toward... At the same time that you are moving away from mere biblical knowledge in Milestone #5, you are moving toward transformational knowing; toward having, by God's grace, a more Christlike character; and toward the integration of faith and practice—toward congruency of belief and behavior; a comprehensive Christian world view; a master motive, a God-given goal that orients and orders your entire life and grants it meaning; and embodying or incarnating God's Word.

Readiness for the Milestone #5

Children's capacity for understanding and processing biblical and moral concepts is limited and they need to respond to biblical truths on their own levels. We must therefore be careful not to expect or demand adult understanding from children. But with adolescence "thinking takes wings." A young person can now begin to think about thinking, is capable of deductive logic ("If... then..."), can form generalizations, and does abstract thinking. Adolescents are capable of looking beyond their immediate experience and examining various alternatives and solutions. Simple answers are no longer sufficient, so they ask, "Why?" or "What for?" [1]
This level of thinking allows adolescents to consider key questions about life, and then construct a system of personal biblical beliefs and meaning.

This more complex level of thinking is new for adolescents, and they will need to continue to develop these skills as they enter adulthood and throughout their lifespan. Keep in mind, however, that not all adults regularly perform at this level. Also, theorists suggest that certain types of thinking are unique to adulthood. These may include accepting conflict, pragmatic problem-solving, and understanding paradox. [2] These changes in the way we think come with time and experience.

Hear now the wise words of J. I. Packer on the importance of God's written Word:

> Why has God spoken? The truly staggering answer which the Bible gives to this question is that God's purpose in revelation is to make friends with us. It was to this end that He created us rational beings, bearing His image, able to think and hear and speak and love. He wanted there to be genuine personal affection and friendship, two-sided, between Himself and us—a relation, not like that between a man and a dog, but like that of a father and a son, or a husband to his wife. Loving friendship between two persons has no ulterior motive; it is an end in itself. And this is God's end in revelation. He speaks to us simply to fulfill the purpose for which we were made; that is, to bring into being a relationship in which He is a friend to us, and we to Him. [3]

Having read what contemporary believer J.I. Packer has written about God's Word, now consider what first-century believers and New Testament writers John and Paul had to say about linking truth and life.

The Apostle John on God's Word

"I have written to you, young men, because... the Word of God abides in you" (1 John 2:14). The verb *abide* refers to an inward, enduring personal communion. Used twenty two times in 1 John, *abide* means to settle down, be at home, and remain. The tense of the word in Greek communicates that the abiding of God's Word in believers—and therefore our learning—is ongoing.

Obedience: Seeing Jesus Despite His Absence

The night before Jesus was to be crucified, He assured His eleven faithful disciples that their relationship with Him would continue even though He would physically die. He said, "In My Father's house are many dwelling places... I go to prepare a place for you" (John 14:2), and "If anyone loves Me, he will keep My word; and My Father will love him, and We will come to him, and make Our abode with him" (John 14:23), and the Greek word for "dwelling place" and "abode" is one and the same. The two-fold truth expressed in these verses is, first, the fact that Jesus (interestingly, a skilled carpenter by trade) was returning to heaven to prepare a future residence for the disciples to inhabit with Him later.

Second, as His words in verse 23 reveal, Jesus was also crafting a residence within the earthly life of the believer in the present. What does Jesus do to prepare an abode in His followers? Jesus explained it this way, "He who has My commandments and keeps them, he it is who loves Me; and he who loves Me will be loved by My Father, and I will love him, and will disclose Myself to him" (John 14:21). Though Jesus is physically gone, as we obey His Word, He settles down, and makes Himself at home in us. Obedient believers will experience fresh revelations of Jesus and new insights into the Father's love. Milestone #5 is all about developing this obedient relationship so that, despite Jesus' physical absence from this earth, you are still in an exciting dynamic relationship with Him! In Milestone #5 the believer is experiencing God's Word firsthand as it makes the fourteen inch journey from the head to the heart.

 In John 14:21, Jesus promised to "disclose Myself" to the person who shows love for Jesus by obeying Him. Share a time when acting in obedience to God's Word, you experienced a fresh glimpse of Jesus. Be specific.

We will now consider two dimensions of knowing: objective and subjective, the head and the heart. It is imperative for the Christ follower to see this distinction and to understand the relationship of the two kinds of knowledge to each other. A word of caution: we cannot neglect or overemphasize either dimension without toxic side effects. The two must be kept in balance as we shape a truly authentic Christian faith.

First one dimension of knowing focuses on the content of a biblically informed faith. This is faith viewed as a *noun*: the what of faith ("My commandments"- John 14:21; "My word"- John 14:23). God's truth is to form the framework of a biblical spirituality, but the goal is not Information. The goal of this kind of knowing is Transformation. Second is the experiential side of knowing that is personal; it focuses on owning one's faith and applying it to the particulars of life. This knowledge is formed by lived experience. This is faith viewed as a *verb*: the why and how of faith ("has My commandments and keeps them" - verse 21).

Note carefully that verses 21 and 23 uniquely tie both dimensions together. Although He will be absent from the disciples, Jesus will reveal Himself, show Himself, disclose Himself, make Himself known to them experientially—to the one who shows love for Jesus by obeying Him.

2 ✎ When our head knowledge and our heart knowledge are in balance, knowing God is very real and very exciting. In which of these two dimensions do you want to grow? Explain why—and ideas for what you will do to grow.

Anointed: The Holy Spirit as Tutor

As you probably know, the Holy Spirit is actively involved in your spiritual growth. John the apostle explained it this way: "But you have an anointing from the Holy One, and you all know. As for you, the anointing which you received from Him abides in you, and you have no need for any one to teach you; but as His anointing teaches you about all things" (1 John 2:20,27). Just as Old Testament kings and priests were anointed to fulfill their roles in God's kingdom, every single New testament believer (and that includes you and me!) is anointed with the Holy Spirit at salvation. The Holy Spirit—with whom we are anointed—plays a crucial role in our spiritual growth. One of His responsibilities, for instance, is to be every believer's Resident Tutor. Note that John was *not* saying that Christians don't need teachers. After all, John himself taught with these very words in his letter! John was, however, emphasizing that believer don't need to rely only on others for learning God's truth, understanding His Word, and applying it to life. Our Resident Tutor helps us discover on our own the meaning and application of the Scriptures. Believers in the Young Adulthood stage of faith will come to be governed by the Scriptures, and stop looking to the group or significant others as their primary authority.

The Apostle Paul on God's Word

Now let's see what the apostle Paul taught about the role of God's written Word in our journey of faith. We'll look at 1 Corinthians as a case study of spiritual immaturity. What was the reason for the Corinthians' spiritual dwarfism? According to Paul, they were lacking an ever-deepening, and life-changing knowledge of God's Word. Believers know God's Word at different levels: some know Scriptures firsthand and others simply don't. In 1 Corinthians Paul contrasted the "spiritual" believer and the "infant" believer, and discussed the place of God's Word plays in the lives of each.

The "Spiritual" Believer

In 1 Corinthians 2:15 Paul wrote, "But he who is spiritual appraises all things, yet he himself is appraised by no man." Paul was not referring to an elite group of advanced Christians when he wrote about "he who is spiritual." Paul was simply referring to people who are controlled by, and led by the Holy Spirit, and this passage says three things about such a person.

1. A spiritual person "appraises all things," and appraise is a legal term that means to bring to trial before the presiding judge who examines all the evidence. The appraisal is the questioning process—the investigation, the cross-examination—that precedes the verdict. This analogy teaches that a spiritual person's faith is meaningful because he/she constantly examines and applies God's truth to personal and pressing real-life situations. Spiritual people appraise "all things"; they exercise discernment on a broad range of issues that affect their own spiritual

growth as well as their day-to-day life. How unlike the infant Corinthian Christians whose lives, values, attitudes, and beliefs were largely unexamined.

2. A spiritual person "is appraised by no man." Spiritual people are able to stand alone, looking and answering only to God. Their life is shaped by self-chosen principles from God's Word—regardless of what others think. Spiritual people are not motivated by external approval, the need to conform, or the desire to compete with others. Motivated only by the truth of God's Word, spiritual people own their faith. Again, in sharp contrast are the baby Corinthian Christians who let Apollos, Cephas, and Paul do their thinking for them (1 Corinthians 1:12; 3:4). These infants in the faith listened to their heroes of the faith and conformed to their ideas in order to win their approval. Consequently these babies experienced little spiritual growth and they didn't come close to owning a firsthand faith.

3. A spiritual person increasingly has "the mind of Christ" (1 Corinthians 2:16). Thinking the way Christ think happens more and more for believers who appraise all things and then stand alone when their understanding of the truth leads them to a faith they truly own. The infant Corinthian believers did not have the mind of Christ; they had only the wisdom of man (2:5,8,9).

3 ✎ An appraisal—an investigation, a cross-examination—of what you believe will strengthen your faith. What aspect(s) of your faith might be an appropriate focus of some appraisal?

The "Infant" Believer
The picture of a mature believer may become more striking as you contrast it to the following 1 Corinthians sketch of an infant Christian—a person who is controlled and led by the flesh. As you read about these baby Christians whose infancy was unduly prolonged and whose growth was stunted look for reasons for this immaturity. First Corinthians 3:1-4 identifies five characteristics of spiritual immaturity and, in doing so, teaches much about healthy growth.

1. Three to five years after their salvation, these adult Corinthians were still infants in their faith. Their behavior was indistinguishable from the natural man (2:13) who never claimed to be a Christian. Normal spiritual growth had not occurred (3:2,3), childish characteristics persisted, and as his words suggest ("Not yet... even now... still"), Paul was furious! Clearly, spiritual growth is not automatic, nor does the passing of time guarantee progress.

2. The Corinthian Christians have chosen a deficient diet. Paul wrote, "I gave you milk to drink, not solid food" (3:2). Mother's milk is essential to normal growth, but soon solid foods must be added to ensure healthy development. Milk alone would be insufficient. Likewise, spiritual infancy is nourished by milk, but the Corinthians were stuck at that infant stage. They had failed to move on to solid food, so they had missed out on "God's wisdom" (1 Corinthians 2:7), "the depths of God" (2:10), and "the mind of Christ" (2:16), three results of growth that are at the same time keys to further growth.

3. Despite their advancing chronological age, the Corinthians are "not yet able" to ingest solid food (3:2). The Corinthian believers were not simply ignorant and in need of more information. Rather, their beliefs had not affected their behavior. Paul asked ten times, "Do you not know?" (3:16; 5:6; 6:2, 3, 9, 15, 16, 19; 9:13, 24). The Corinthians failed to apply what they already knew. They did not "appraise" the issues they faced or try to live out what they already knew. In other words, they did not ingest their food. The food simply passed through their bodies without contributing to their growth.

4. Another reason for the Corinthian Christians' spiritual immaturity was their reliance on other people or groups. They were conformists, choosing to follow leaders like Paul, Apollos, or Cephas (1:12; 3:4) and letting these authorities do their thinking for them. The Corinthians did not own their faith; theirs was borrowed and secondhand. They were not abiding in the Word of God, or they were not expecting Scripture to impact their faith and inform their life.

5. The Corinthians' relationships with one another did not provide the mix of support and challenge necessary to spark and sustain spiritual growth. Unresolved interpersonal conflicts, described by Paul as "jealousy and strife" (3:3), were rampant. This explains Paul's emphasis on building community in 1 Corinthians 12-14.

Where, if at all, do you see yourself in this description of the infant Christian?

Through Paul's words about infant Christians, what is God calling you to do?

Levels of Learning God's Word

As we've looked at the first five milestones on the journey of faith, we've seen the need to consider not only the content of our Christian beliefs and values, but also the process by which we came to our beliefs and values. Looking at how we learn about anything can help us understand how we come to a more mature faith in Jesus.

Learning takes place on the following levels:

1. Memorizing facts
2. Understanding principles
3. Realizing implications of facts and principles for life
4. Choosing to obey now within the learner's reach
5. Changing one's behavior. [4]

Similarly, the Word of God "abides" in believers at differing levels, each one more transformative in its effects than the previous one. We can learn the Bible on any and all of these levels, but only at the "Realization" level, when the Word of God most fully "abides" in us, does it transform our lives. Learning God's Word at any lower level is unlikely to change your life.

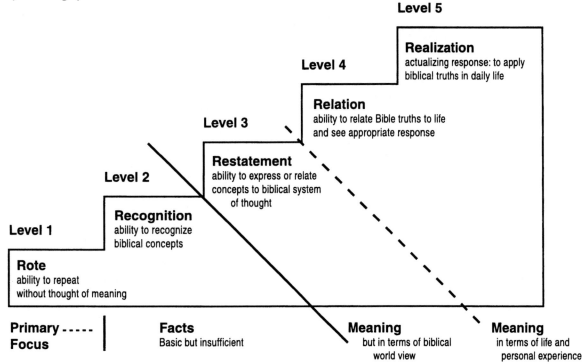

5 What percentage of your biblical learning experience has been at Level 1 or 2? Why do you think that's the case?

What may be keeping you from advancing to Level 3 and beyond?

Extent of Learning God's Word

Remember that in Milestone #5 the Word of God is to be increasingly integrated into our experience—and this process is to continue through life. Educators Habermas and Issler identify three domains in which learning takes place and we are to grow and improve—by degree—in each of these domains. [5]

1. Cognition, the domain of knowledge—
  Part of learning is knowing.
      Degree 1: Awareness
      Degree 2: Understanding
      Degree 3: Wisdom

2. Conviction, the domain of attitudes, values, and emotions—
  Part of learning touches one at the level of feelings and motivations.
      Degree 1: Expressed by sensitivity to others
      Degree 2: Expressed by empathy
      Degree 3: Expressed by compassion in action

3. Competence, the domain of physical skill and habits—
  Part of learning is linked to how skilled one is in using what is learned.
      Degree 1: Accomplished with some difficulty
      Degree 2: Accomplished with ease
      Degree 3: Accomplished with improvisation

The Word of God abides in believers in each domain but to differing degrees. As we grow, we will become more accomplished in each domain of cognition, conviction, and competence—areas that I liken to the Head, the Heart, and the Hands. As we mature in the faith, we will also move toward Wisdom (head), Compassion in action (heart), and Serving with improvisation (hands).

Four Milestones along the Journey of Faith

Review the ten Characteristics of Stages of Faith from pages 13-14. In the fourth premise, we learned not only that the stages of faith can fuel one another, but that they also have the power to delay our spiritual progress. Unfinished work on Milestones #1-#4, for instance, will keep you from moving beyond the Childhood stage of faith and prevent the Word of God from fully abiding in you. In light of that fact, let's briefly review Milestones #1-#4. At each milestone, notice how genuine efforts there can catalyze growth at Milestone #5, where you are learning to let God's Word both guide and transform you.

Milestone #1, Experiencing God's Grace and Forgiveness: In Milestone #1 you move toward grace-based living, confident in God's certain, unconditional and nonrepayable love. You learn to let go of pretense and be real. Now, as you read the Bible, you will hear the words without condemnation. There is a compelling attraction to know and follow His Word.

Milestone #2 Embracing God as Father: In Milestone #2, you move toward trust and full surrender to God as *Abba*, Daddy. He is utterly reliable, completely safe, and absolutely trustworthy. As you read the Bible, then, you are drawn to relationship with Him, and you want to please Him regardless of the cost.

Milestone #3 Growing Up Together: In Milestone #3, you move toward relationships with fellow believers whom you select to wash your dirty feet. These people will offer you an empowering mix of support and challenge as you wash their feet and they wash your feet. These special friends will be there to cheer you on toward the Christlikeness you read about in the Bible.

Milestone #4 Owning a Firsthand Faith: In Milestone #4, you move toward firsthand, owned faith and internalized convictions. Regardless of what the group thinks, you stand alone and with confidence about your well-grounded biblical faith. After all, as you've read in the Bible, transformation involves examining and revising your beliefs and values so that your faith is your own.

Your Guide: The Mentoring Parent

At each step of your spiritual journey, you will benefit from the insight and experience of someone who has already traveled this road. Such a Parent in the faith would have worked through Milestone #5 and be linking God's truth to his/her life. The Parent is not merely a model or a moralizer. Instead, the Parent pushes us to think at higher levels and encourages us to move beyond gathering information to experiencing transformation. As one who is a testimony to the power of God's Word, the Parent is qualified to share his/her personal story and guide you on your spiritual journey.

Pilgrims in Progress

Young Adults who are growing in the faith move beyond simply knowing about Scripture to the exciting point of integrating God's Word into daily life. Linking God's truth to one's life gradually transforms the whole person into a more mature and more Christlike believer.

  One point from this lesson that will motivate me to learn God's Word at the next higher level is...

Reflect on how well you are linking God's truth, as revealed in His written Word, to your daily life. Where might His truth inform your thoughts? Modify your actions? In what ways are you *not* living out or living according to God's truth? Ask the Holy Spirit to help you answer these questions.

A Closing Prayer

God, I come before You aware of how much I have to learn and experience about You.... Thank You that You give me Your Word so that I can know You better... and forgive me for being satisfied with keeping that knowledge at the level of my head and not letting it penetrate to the level of my convictions and actions.... God, learning means changing, and change can be hard for me.... May I trust Your love as well as Your power to transform me as I move toward letting my knowledge of You impact the way I live.... And, God, make me thirsty for Your Word... and willing and able to apply it to my life.... I pray in Jesus' name. Amen.

Milestone #6 Defeating the Enemies of Spiritual Growth

The Young Adulthood Stage:
The Ownership of Faith

Milestone #4

Owning a Firsthand Faith
To grow spiritually, I need to establish ownership of a distinct, personal faith. Having worked through Milestones #1, #2, and #3, I now have a healthy foundation on which to continue to build my faith. My need to conform will diminish as I rely on biblical principles and values I have examined and internalized as my own.

Milestone #5

Linking Truth and Life
To grow spiritually, I need to allow God's Word to transform me. I will therefore move beyond merely receiving head knowledge from the Bible to, by the power of the Holy Spirit, applying its truth to my life. The Word of God will reside in me and have a centering and guiding influence on me.

Milestone #6

Defeating the Enemies of Spiritual Growth
To grow spiritually, I need to understand the lethal strategy of my three arch enemies—the world, the flesh, and the devil—and be willing to do battle against each of them. Knowing that healthy spiritual growth is impaired by neglecting or inadequately completing the milestones of spiritual development, I will also work on the core issues they address.

Spiritual growth is a long journey toward the goal of becoming "like Christ" (1 John 3:2). Three enemies that jeopardize our journey toward spiritual maturity and wholeness are the focus of the final milestone of Young Adulthood. In Lesson #1, when you were introduced to the "Enemies of Spiritual Growth" (1 John 2:15-17), you discovered that spiritual growth can be impaired and delayed by a conflict with two outside enemies—the world and the devil—as well as by an inner conflict with one's own flesh. These enemies never stop whispering in your ear that you will be happier if you could just have a little more—and this often urgent drive and accompanying sense of dissatisfaction cause believers needless suffering and loss of joy.

Furthermore, these enemies are with us wherever we are on the journey toward spiritual wholeness, and you and I are never too mature to be seduced by them. We can take no vacation from our struggle against these adversaries! At every step of our journey, and in every stage of our growth, these rivals conspire to block the Childhood milestones of the Birth of Faith, the Young Adulthood milestones of the Ownership of Faith, and the Parenthood milestones of Modeling Faith. Since spiritual growth is never automatic, it is important for us to identify our own particular vulnerabilities, hurts, habits, and hungerings. Then we can more easily and more fully yield to God's presence, power, and purposes.

Aims of Lesson #10

Plan to spend about two hours completing this lesson and preparing for your small-group time—but don't be surprised if you slow down at certain points and find yourself spending additional minutes on this material. Many believers—and you may be one of them—have either not had a chance or chosen not to face their spiritual enemies. During your time of personal study, you will:

- ◆ Learn more about the three enemies of spiritual progress and their strategies
- ◆ Discover points at which you are vulnerable to these three enemies
- ◆ Learn how you can defeat these enemies
- ◆ Review the Young Adulthood stage of faith
- ◆ Identify what you have yet to do in the Young Adulthood stage of faith

For Small-Group Leaders:

We recommend that during the ninety-minute study portion of this meeting, group members discuss the following questions.

Lesson 10
1, 3-5, 7-9

You will not be able to give equal time to each question above. So, as group leader, budget your time carefully.

☑ Note:

Before reading through this Milestone, take a moment to glance at your **Spiritual Growth Profile**. Looking briefly at that mirror to your spiritual journey will help you put the coming discussion into the more personal context of your own spiritual growth.

Retracing Our Steps

We have looked at two of the three milestones that characterize the Young Adulthood stage of faith. Milestone #4 has challenged you to move past an affiliative style/synthetic-conventional stage of faith to a personally owned faith-life. Milestone #5 focused on the centering and transforming influence of God's Word. Key to linking God's Word to your life (Milestone #5) is having worked on Milestone #4 (as well as attended to Milestones #1-3). Otherwise, Milestone #5 will be muffled and minimized in your experience.

Overview of Milestone #6
Defeating the Enemies of Spiritual Growth

— "War is not something that illustrates aspects of Christian living. Christian living is warfare."
— "All who attempt for a single day to lead a life centered on God and His kingdom will discover that they have a
battle on their hands."

Perhaps the metaphor surprises you, but spiritual growth truly is a battle—and rest assured that the inevitable conflict is not a result of lack of faith. Whether you are a Child, a Young Adult, or a Parent in your faith, you can be sure that three enemies are working to sabotage your journey. The world, the flesh, and the devil compete for your loyalties, your energy, and your trust. These three deadly enemies conspire to block the growth that can be sparked by working through the 1 John milestones that we're looking at. Threats to your purity as well as your progress, these enemies strive to thwart spiritual growth in the Childhood and Young Adulthood stages, thus curtailing the formation of mature, seasoned, mentoring Parents in the faith.

None of our opponents, however, is omnipotent or unbeatable. We can therefore have courage in the Lord, boldly confront the conflicts and challenges that come our way, and continue to grow toward wholeness and Christlikeness. The apostle John neither sensationalized nor minimized spiritual warfare in our Christian life, and he also made it clear that growth is never automatic.

 Based on 1 John 2:13-14 ("I am writing to you, young men, because you have overcome the evil one"), Milestone #6 addresses the core issue of a lived-out faith in God triumphing over the world, the flesh, and the devil. The truth to be learned here is: "I can recognize and counter each of the three enemies which threaten my spiritual growth."

 **Moving Away From...** In Milestone #6 you are working on moving away from the powerful influences of the world, the flesh, and the devil—from these three enemies that assault you from within and without; and from bondage, compulsive drives, subtle and not-so-subtle deceptions, irrational beliefs, and points of vulnerability to these enemies, all of which jeopardize your growth toward Christlikeness.

 **Moving Toward...** At the same time that you are moving away from the influence of the world, the flesh, and the devil in Milestone #6, you are working toward overcoming these enemies' efforts to undermine your personal holiness and wholeness—toward victory over the world, the flesh, and the devil; toward becoming a dynamic and authentic believer; and toward the freedom that comes from yielding oneself fully to God.

Warfare on Three Fronts

John identified the three stages of spiritual development in 1 John 2:12-14. In the verses that immediately follow, he focused on the three enemies to such growth—the world, the flesh, and the evil one. Then, in 2:18-27, John warned of the presence of darkness and deception active in this "last hour."

13 I am writing to you, young men, because you have overcome the evil one... 15 Do not love the world, nor the things in the world. If anyone loves the world, the love of the Father is not in him. 16 For all that is in the world, the lust of the flesh and the lust of the eyes and the boastful pride of life, is not from the Father, but is from the world. 17 The world is passing away, and also its lusts; but the one who does the will of God lives forever.

Our three enemies—the world, the flesh, and the devil—form a trinity of evil and conspire to lure us off the path as we travel through the Parenthood stage of faith and toward Christlike wholeness. Along the way, we find ourselves assaulted by outside forces (the world system and the devil) as well as inner forces (the flesh: "the lust of the flesh and the lust of the eyes and the boastful pride of life"). At every step of the journey, we must be alert to the strategies of our enemies. If unchecked, their efforts will lead us off the path, and we'll find ourselves disillusioned, disappointed, and exhausted.

3 Rivals conspire to block the process of becoming "like Him."

Ready for Battle

During World War II General George Patton led his troops and tanks in a successful counterattack against German forces led by General Erwin Rommel. At the height of the battle, Patton is reported to have shouted, "I read your book, Rommel! I read your book!" And that he had. In his book *Infantry Attacks*, Rommel had carefully outlined his military strategy. Having read his enemies' book, Patton knew what to expect and planned his moves accordingly. Like Patton, Young Adults in the faith honestly identify their vulnerabilities in order to shore up those weaknesses. Then, led and empowered by the Holy Spirit, Young Adults are prepared to face all three enemies.

John Stott describes the "young men" in conflict, overcoming areas where sin's power has been present.

> The young men are busily involved in the battle of Christian living. The Christian life, then, is not just enjoying the forgiveness and the fellowship of God, but fighting the enemy. The forgiveness of past sins must be followed by deliverance from sin's present power, justification followed by sanctification. So in both messages to the young men it is asserted that they have overcome (NEB, "mastered") the evil one. Their conflict has become a conquest. [1]

Enemy #1: The World - Outer Conflict

Programmed to Conform

Six times in verses 15-17, the apostle John referred to the world, to "the life of human society as organized under the power of evil." The word John used for world (cosmos) refers to the culture and age we live in—its ungodly values, attitudes, models, messages, and life-styles. Clearly, we Christians live in an environment hostile to God.

Through the process of socialization or enculturation, we thoughtlessly absorb the values and perspectives of our culture and we are powerfully shaped—and misshaped—by them. The secular world system conditions us and even programs us to conform to its ways; it desensitizes, entangles, entices, pollutes, and distracts. The growing Christian must therefore rely on the truth revealed in Scriptures in order to recognize and stand strong against the culture's many counterfeits.

In the West, for instance, we must battle the influences of our increasingly secular culture that values achievement (status), acquisition (affluence), appearance, and self-sufficiency. In this contemporary pluralistic culture, we must counter postmodern moral relativism (the stance that there are no truths that apply in every time, in every place, and to every person), its virtue of tolerance, and its commitment to rationalism. These warped and twisted values and the corresponding pressure to conform to them compete with God's truth, numb our need for Him, muffle His voice, and often derail our progress toward maturity and Christlikeness. The Young Adult, however, is skilled at identifying these toxic influences.

 Which influences of your own culture are you most susceptible to? Explain.

God is uncompromising in His command to us to not love the world (1 John 2:15). We Christians are to love God (2:5) and our brothers and sisters (2:10), but we are not to love the world. Love for the world is incompatible with love for the Father. Furthermore, as John pointed out, this world is passing away (2:17). We are to as resist the powerful influences of its fleeting values and instead embraces the eternal values of God.

Consider T.S. Eliot's epitaph for those people who deem spiritual matters irrelevant:

> Here were a decent godless people:
> Their only monument the asphalt road
> And a thousand lost golf balls.

 What do the following verses teach about Enemy #1, the world?

John 14:27 . Ephesians 2:2

Romans 12:2 James 4:4

 What will you do to "overcome" the world when you find its values in conflict with your spiritual growth? Be specific.

Enemy #2: The Flesh - Inner Conflict

Chronic Dissatisfaction

The Bible offers countless illustrations of our twisted, tangled human nature, and God's commands are intended to help us curb our restless, instinct-driven heart and habits. Each of us can all too easily be energized by dark desires and motives and guided by distorted ideas about God, His world, and ourselves. Enemy #1 (the world) and Enemy #3 (the devil) capitalize on that fact and conspire together with Enemy #2, our sinful nature, to block our spiritual growth and compete for the control of our lives. This enemy's strategy is rooted in the chronic and sinful dissatisfaction within the believer's soul. (As George Bernard Shaw observed, "There are two tragedies in life. One is not to get what you want. The other is to get it.")

In the Young Adult stage of faith, believers become skilled in standing strong against the pursuit of sensual pleasure, the urge to acquire, and the desire for recognition. The word lust means "strong desire" and suggests compulsions, indulgent habits, urges, hungerings, and longings too strong to resist—without the Lord's help. Furthermore, addictions to our desires and appetites will actually deprive us of freedom, joy, and, of course, our spiritual growth. Lust is lying when it tells you that you need, deserve, or are entitled to more and that you will be happy when you have more. A mature Christian realizes that the fulfillment of our appetites will not truly satisfy.

"The lust of the flesh"

"I want what will feel good"—The lust of the flesh is the desire for *sensual* pleasure. Fueled by hormones and compulsive habits, the lust of the flesh leads to self-indulgence and a short-lived high. The focus is on gratifying legitimate needs in illegitimate ways, and the preoccupation is self-fulfillment.

"The lust of the eyes"

"I want what I see" —The lust of the eyes is the desire for *acquisitional* pleasure. We all know the appeal of material things and how easy it is to be captivated by the outward appearance pressured by marketing, peers, and the burning desire to keep up with the Joneses. In our "obey your thirsts" culture, our wants become needs, and we deify material things. It's easy to want what we see without considering their fleeting, superficial value (1 John 2:17).

"The boastful pride of life"

"I want to be first—and I better be anything but last!" —The boastful pride of life is the desire for *recognitional* pleasure. This desire to be significant, affirmed, worthwhile, or admired can easily lead to drivenness, narcissism, and the tyrannical need to excel. Striving for achievement, control, power, prestige, and status fosters self-promotion and self-exaltation.

 To which of these internal enemies— the pursuit of sensual pleasure, the urge to acquire, and the desire for recognition—are you most vulnerable? Explain why you answered as you did—and even why you think you are most vulnerable to that enemy. Identify one consequence of this vulnerability and its impact on you and others.

Read the following verses and record what you learn about the flesh, Enemy #2.

Jeremiah 17:9   Galatians 5:16-17

Mark 4:18-19   1 Peter 2:11

 Now figure out what you will do to stand strong against these internal enemies, especially the one that attacks you most persistently. Be specific and biblical in your battle plan.

Enemy #3: The Devil - Outer Conflict

Architect of Deception

The "evil one" (2:13) is the pernicious mastermind behind the forces of the world (conformity) and the flesh (chronic dissatisfaction), and he plots to undermine a believer's growth in Christlikeness. Satan's lies and deceptions are designed to keep believers from ever being mature Parents in the faith. During the Young Adulthood Stage of faith, however, believers become more skilled at recognizing and overcoming their enemies to Christlikeness.

6 In order to more quickly recognize and more easily overcome the devil, record what the following verses teach about him.

2 Corinthians 11:14   1 Peter 5:8-9

Ephesians 6:11,12,16   1 John 4:4; 5:19

 7 What will you do now to stand strong against and even defeat the evil one? Be specific.

Breaking the Enemies' Chains: Taking Steps to Freedom

As we have seen, we Christians are the target of the world, the flesh, and the evil one. So we Christians have to learn that God needs full control of our lives as well as of thoughts, words, and deeds. That's why, in the Young Adult stage of faith, believers come clean about any areas where appetites or habits have a hold on them. This truth-telling is one step in the process of overcoming the evil in one's life. We Christians also overcome the enemies of our soul when we are driven to despair, brokenness, confession, repentance, and the choice to trust God and fully yield to His truth, His control, and His healing.

8 In what area of your life do you want to break free of the enemies' chains and experience victory where you are their target? Then personalize the steps just listed as a prayer in which you express your fresh surrender and obedience to God.

The Battleground

Even as God's Holy Spirit uses the eight milestones of spiritual growth to encourage your journey toward Christlikeness, your three enemies are conspiring to slow, if not completely prevent, your growth.

In each column below you'll find listed those harmful influences that the milestones of spiritual development can help believers move away from. Circle those items that you think the enemies of your soul are using today to sabotage your spiritual growth.

Milestone #1
Experiencing Grace and Forgiveness

Inadequate understanding of God's grace
Incomplete experience of God's healing
Tyranny of oughts and shoulds
Self-condemnation, self-justification
Identity not based on God's love

Milestone #2
Embracing God as Father

Distorted perceptions of God
God of the head separated from God of the heart
Professed beliefs about God without felt-sense of God.

Milestone #3
Growing Up Together

Impoverished relationships
Proximity without community
Superficial relationships
Isolation, independence
Dependence on people for security and worth
Absence of mentoring Parent

Milestone #4
Owning a Firsthand Faith

Secondhand faith
Faith weakened by external conventions
Conformity, compliance
Fictitious sins
Affiliative faith

Milestone #5
Linking Truth to Life

Abstract theology without biography
Information without transformation
Truth accepted but not experienced
Stuck at lower levels of learning

Milestone #6
Defeating the Enemies of Spiritual Progress

Naivete about the three enemies—the world, the flesh, the devil
Crippled by forces that condition and conform us to live as the world lives

Milestone #7
Empowering Others

Doing for others what they can do for themselves
Cloning disciples
Negligence of care-giving

Milestone #8
Seasoned by Time and Experience

Stagnation
Resignation
Lack of motivation to grow

Your Guide: The Mentoring Parent

At each step of your spiritual journey, you will benefit from the insight and experience of someone who has traveled this road. Seasoned Parents in the faith would have worked through Milestone #6 and know how to stand strong against the enemies of spiritual progress. They can help you learn to identify the deceptions and strategies of your adversaries—the world, the flesh, and the devil. Parents in the faith help you move away from bondage, vulnerabilities, compulsions, deceptions, irrational beliefs, and superficialities that jeopardize your spiritual growth, and they can help you move toward a healthy, authentic, and contagious faith.

A Review of the Young Adulthood Stage of Faith

The work on the Young Adulthood milestones must be done if you are to move toward owning an adult faith, and living openly and honestly in the light, grounded in and guided by God's truth. Like the three Childhood milestones, the milestones of Young Adulthood cannot be neglected without diminishing your spiritual health and aggravating your growth toward Christlikeness. Attending to the three milestones of Young Adulthood will lead to a consistent, coherent, and owned faith. Furthermore, your work at this stage will determine the quality and health of your spiritual progress in the Parenthood stage.

But looking at why you believe what you say you believe—the challenging task at the heart of Young Adulthood—is certain to bring discomfort and maybe even crisis. That examination of your beliefs may be painful, but it can also mean a renewal of your faith, as well as a new and solid direction for your life as you live with Jesus at the center. This sort of stretching is essential to an adult's ownership of the faith—a faith that is healing, freeing, penetrating, intimate, and transforming. This kind of faith leads to knowing true joy in the Lord (1 John 1:4).

Remember that the Young Adulthood stage of faith is not to be confused with chronological adolescence. Spiritual growth at this level is not characteristic of people even in their early twenties. Some people may reach the stage of Young Adulthood in their mid-twenties, but the early thirties are more likely. Many adults, however, reach a plateau at the Young Adulthood stage of their journey of faith. Too many adults get stuck and never move on to the Parenthood stage. Why does this happen? Consider some factors:

Expectations for growth that are too high: Believers are pushed, hurried on, and pressured into bigger and better spiritual activities and/or goals at a pace that doesn't fit with their unique personal timetable. Burnout causes stalling. Inattention to Childhood's three milestones also has serious side effects on Milestones #4, #5, and #6.

Expectations for growth that are too low: Sometimes believers receive insufficient support and/or challenge from the Christian community, so they don't know there's room to grow or what to do to grow. Also, often believers don't have a Parent in the faith to serve as mentor and guide.

Bland religious teaching: Well-intentioned but poorly executed church, Sunday-school, and parental teaching can fail to develop our critical thinking skills. Learning environments that lack warmth, enthusiasm, and people with contagious faith in Jesus also contribute to the stalling of Christian growth.

Rigidity: Some churches emphasize external performance, conditional acceptance, and doctrinal profession but don't give individuals the opportunity to evaluate their faith, wrestle with hard questions, and come to the point of owning their Christian convictions. The entire process that leads to owning one's faith never even has a chance to begin.

Sinful choices: One reason sin so effectively prevents spiritual growth is that it blinds us to its paralyzing consequences. We can never know the full and far-reaching effects of our sin on our spiritual growth. We must also remember that we can fall at any point of our journey of faith.

The comfort of Affiliative Faith: All of us want to belong and be accepted. That's one reason why believers choose, consciously or otherwise, to stay at the level of Affiliative Faith. When we begin to evaluate our faith and search out answers to hard questions, we may find the journey lonely, uncomfortable, even a little frightening.

■ ■ ■

Each believer has his or her own timetable for spiritual growth, and God promises that He is at work in each Christian (Philippians 1:6). And it's good to remember that He has a limitless number of creative ways to get a Christian—to get *you*—moving forward again.

The Three Milestones of the Young Adulthood Stage of Faith
The following summary presents the goals of the important milestones of Young Adulthood.

Milestone #4 — Owning a Firsthand Faith
I am self-governing and able to determine my own values and convictions apart from people who are important to me but whose ideas may be different. I continue to need the support and challenge of other believers, but I am no longer dependent on them to tell me what to believe, to show me how to behave, or to approve of my values and beliefs. By examining my faith, I come to own it, and my owned and internalized faith leads me to live according to God's principles.

If I were to neglect this milestone, I would remain a weak Christian, motivated primarily by the need to conform and comply and by the desire to win the approval of people I deem significant. My critical-thinking skills would stay undeveloped, and my obedience to God would remain mechanical, obligatory and burdensome.

Milestone #5 — Linking Truth to Life

My faith is congruent with my life; my talk matches my walk. God's Word has become internalized and is the centering, orienting influence for all that I do.

If I were to neglect this milestone, my life would be one of orthodoxy rather than an incarnation of God's love and truth. I would merely accept God's truth rather than experiencing its power. The lordship of Jesus Christ would merely be a matter of cognition and creed rather than the foundation for my life.

Milestone #6 — Defeating the Enemies of Spiritual Growth

I am well aware that spiritual growth occurs on a battleground, not a playground. The powerful forces of the world, the flesh, and the devil seek to conform and condition me, but I have learned to recognize and overcome each of these enemies.

If I were to neglect this milestone, I would be unprepared and unprotected in the inevitable and ongoing spiritual battle that surrounds believers. I would find myself still vulnerable to the strategies of my enemies.

Throughout your life, you will continue to grow in dimensions of faith marked by the Young Adulthood milestones. Remember that time spent on these milestones will both keep ritualism from setting in to your relationship with God and keep you owning your faith. Keep in mind, too, that your three enemies never slumber—but neither does your Shield and Protector.

 In what aspects of your faith are you still in the Young Adulthood? Be specific.

A Closing Prayer

Almighty God, thank You that You give me the power to stand strong against the enemies of my spiritual growth... and thank You that the ultimate victory—the victory won on the Cross—is Yours and, through Jesus Christ, mine as well... God, I ask You to help me stand strong in my faith... Keep me sensitive to the onslaught of the enemies—the world, the flesh, and the devil—especially when their strategy is subtle and alluring.... Thank You for Your promises to be with me always.... May I know Your presence with me.... especially where I am powerless, vulnerable, and crippled. I pray in Jesus' name. Amen.

Lesson 11

Milestone #7 Empowering Others

The Parenthood Stage:
Modeling Faith

Milestone #7

Empowering Others
To grow spiritually, I need to assume my responsibility to parent other members of God's family, offering experience from my own spiritual journey and guided by the biblical principles of spiritual growth that are reflected in these milestones of faith. I will work to acquire the skills I need to effectively nurture my brothers and sisters toward Christlikeness and wholeness.

Milestone #8

Seasoned by Time and Experience

What exactly does Christian maturity look like? Remember that spiritual progress is not some sort of private self-actualization. Instead, spiritual progress takes us increasingly in the direction of Christlikeness, and Christlikeness will in turn take us to the place of assuming responsibility for influencing the spiritual growth of fellow believers.

As we've said before, there are no shortcuts to spiritual maturity, but there is an important source of help within the body of Christ. That source is a Parent in the faith, a person who has worked diligently on the eight milestones of spiritual growth— and is therefore uniquely qualified to empower the Child and Young Adult along their own journeys of faith. Parents have traveled far and grown mature in the Christian faith; they can personally testify to God's love and healing and share that story with others. Parents have answered such important questions as "What does it mean to live for Jesus?" and "Is my life about something that matters?"

We have charted the course of faith's journey, but each one of us needs more than a map. We also need the personal guidance and the hard-won wisdom of the Parent. A Parent in the faith is credible and authentic with nothing to prove, no image to maintain, and no facades to preserve. You'll find no hints of stereotypical discipleship efforts to make you a clone of another believer. Instead, the Parent has acquired the skills that will help free you to move toward Christlikeness and toward the wholeness that God designed you to know in Him.

Aims of Lesson #11

Plan to spend about two hours completing this lesson and preparing for your small-group time. During your time of personal study, you will:

◆ Consider what the Parent can do to impact other Christians to grow
◆ Learn what the Bible says about empowering one's fellow believers
◆ Listen for God's call to you to be a care-giver

For Small-Group Leaders:

We recommend that during the ninety-minute study portion of this meeting, group members discuss the following questions.

**Lesson 11
1-8**

You will not be able to give equal time to each question. So, as the group leader, budget your time carefully.

☑ Note:

Before reading through this Milestone, take a moment to glance at your **Spiritual Growth Profile**. Looking briefly at that mirror to your spiritual journey will help you put the coming discussion into the more personal context of your own spiritual growth.

The Parenthood Stage of Spiritual Growth

Where is this lifelong journey of faith taking me? What does spiritual maturity look like? What fruit will these stages of faith and their respective milestones bear?

Around 95 A.D., the apostle John wrote to a first-century church where some people had known Christ for as long as sixty years. These seasoned veterans in the faith had become the fathers or Parents in the Christian faith—and, in some very real ways, these fathers had become like *the* Father. The two remaining milestones in John's stages of faith are mature believers like those John knew.

John addressed the fathers in the faith (1 John 2:13, 14), those individuals who had come to recognize that nothing in this life surpasses knowing Christ intimately and empowering others to do the same. With these two eternal values governing the life of those who are Parents in the faith, these Parents pass on to others the spiritual reality they have come to know deeply and, always looking to the map of stages of faith, guide these fellow believers on their own spiritual journey. Key to the Parents' influence is their personal testimony about God's love, care, and healing.

Milestone #7 — Empowering Others
Milestone #8 — Seasoned by Time and Experience

Constitutionally different from being a Child or Young Adult in the Faith, Parents in the Faith can expect to find the following at this stage of their growth:

◆ **A New Agenda** At Milestone #7 a Parent works to become a skilled guide, a worthy example to imitate, and a bold advocate for other believers traveling the journey toward wholeness and Christlikeness. Parents have moved from hurting, to being healed, to helping. Therefore, each Parent has a powerful and personal story of spiritual growth to share. Later, in Milestone #8, holiness and wholeness most fully merge.

◆ **A New Perspective** Profound changes and growth can continue throughout one's life, and the Parenthood stage marks the culmination of some of these changes. Milestone #7, for instance, climaxes the movement from self-absorption to sacrificial love. Milestone #8 encourages Parents to share the wisdom of their seasoned, rich, and full faith, wisdom that is free of pretense and imbalances, wisdom that only comes only with age and with the real-life experience of an owned, firsthand faith.

◆ **New Dangers** Remember that any unfinished business from Childhood and Young Adulthood will interfere with the milestones of Parenthood. Also consider these four warnings specific to the Parent stage: Don't grow comfortable and let yourself stagnate or retire; don't neglect the next generation of Christians; avoid formulas of discipleship which can too easily result in the superficial production of spiritual clones; and continue to grow in your faith, staying centered in the Lord Jesus Christ.

◆ **A New Invitation** The Child and Young Adult in the faith can benefit greatly from the Parent's spiritual care-giving, and that's the challenging invitation to the mature Christian: to care for the next generation of believers (Milestone #7). Even as the lifelong journey of faith continues for the Parents, they are challenged to face the unfamiliar issues that come with aging (Milestone #8). And of course the Parent continues to work on Milestones #1-#6.

Readiness for the Parenthood Stage of Faith

Since both a substantial length of time of walking with the Lord and a variety of life experiences are prerequisite for spiritual maturity, the stage of Parenthood doesn't begin until at least the mid-thirties. Remember that the Young Adulthood stage is simply beyond the capabilities of the teenager and early adult and is not likely consistent and coherent until after age thirty. If a person has attended to the milestones of Childhood and Young Adulthood, middle-age adulthood is generally the entry level to Parenthood in the faith. Of course we should not wait until middle-aged adulthood to serve others and encourage their growth in the faith. But know that as you mature, you grow in the ability to empower others. Because the Parent in the faith has worked on Milestones #1-#6 through the years, they are uniquely qualified to empower the Child and the Young Adult on their journey.

Overview of Milestone #7
Empowering Others

Based on 1 John 2:13-14 ("I am writing to you, fathers..."), Milestone #7 addresses the core issue of empowering others to grow toward mature faith. This milestone challenges us to guide and nurture others toward wholeness and Christlikeness.

Moving Away From... In Milestone #7, you work on moving away from self-absorption—from avoiding care-giving and neglecting the needs of younger believers; from failing to bear fruit as a believer; from formulas and methods of discipleship that turn out clones rather than believers whose faith reflects their uniqueness and their own personal relationship with Jesus Christ; from using power to control others; from doing for others what they can do for themselves; and from fixing others.

Moving Toward... At the same time, in Milestone #7 you are moving toward sacrificial love—toward offering others the support, challenge, and vision that will spur their growth; toward being able to provide skilled guidance to a Child or Young Adult; toward being a faith-shaper, and wounded healer; toward empowering others; and toward being an example of one who continues to work on the milestones of spiritual growth.

A Guide for the Journey

In the ten lessons so far, we have been developing a map of spiritual progress. Perhaps you've realized that you need more than a map. What you need is a personal, skilled, and experienced guide. A mentoring Parent can be such a sure-footed guide, and your connection with a Parent will be among your most prized relationships in the community of believers.

> Children are the youngest believers, newborn spiritual babes. Young men are those who have had some experience of spiritual conflict. *Fathers* refers to those who have been Christians the longest and have the deepest, ripest, and most mature development. They are the older men in the heavenly family; those who by reason of experience are looked up to for sympathy, guidance, and assistance. [1]

But where are those Parents in the faith who will guide Children or Young Adults in the faith? Tragically, it sems that there are too few men and women who have assumed responsibility to skillfully care for the development of other believers. And one regrettable result of this shortage is that the growth of many believers yet in the Childhood or Young Adulthood stages of faith may be delayed and the faith journey more treacherous.

Two Imperatives for Parents in the faith

First, Parents in the Faith guide others to spiritual birth by skillfully and prayerfully presenting the gospel to the lost. Such personal witness will naturally flow out of a life transformed by Jesus. The seasoned Christian who has experienced God's grace and healing through the years and who knows God's Word firsthand will winsomely share the gospel.

Clearly, our Christian witness is to become more and more effective as we travel toward a mature faith. We see that, for instance, when Jesus talked to His disciples about bearing fruit and described the progression from bearing no fruit, to some fruit, to more fruit, to much fruit (John 15:2, 5, 8). The mature Christian has learned to depend on Christ, the Vine, and therefore produces ripe fruit that will nourish spiritually hungry men and women.

Second, Parents in the faith assume responsibility for guiding other believers toward spiritual growth. They realize that spiritual growth is the process of becoming like Christ *for the sake of others*. [2] While not every Christian may directly lead others to Christ, every Parent in the faith will definitely care for and help guide brothers and sisters who are traveling the road of spiritual growth. Simply put, Parents in the faith are faith-shapers.

Skills of Parents in the faith

Exactly what parenting skills help us empower others toward growth? What does the care-giving of a Parent in the faith look like? What kind of relational skills will the Parent have developed through the years? Paul's ministry offers us answers to these questions. Examine the following verses and note what Paul did to guide fellow believers toward a mature faith.

 1 1 Thessalonians 2:7-8 — List at least three care-giving skills that the "mother" demonstrates.

1 Thessalonians 2:9-11 — List at least three care-giving skills that the "father" might demonstrate.

1 Thessalonians 2:12 — What was Paul's primary vision or objective in his ministry?

Educator Laurent Daloz explores the skills that teachers needed to help students grow, and you'll notice remarkable parallels with Paul's model of care-giving in 1 Thessalonians 2:7-12. [3] Daloz suggests that we guide development by:

▶ Providing support and engendering trust (like the mother in 1 Thessalonians 2:7-8)

▶ I ssuing a challenge (like the father in 1 Thessalonians 2:9-11)

▶ Formulating a vision (for example, "walk in a manner worthy of the God who calls you" from 1 Thessalonians 2:12).

2 Think about your own journey of faith. Who has won your trust and offered you support?

Who has issued you a challenge and thereby spurred your growth? Be specific about what the challenge was and, if possible, the growth that resulted.

Who helped you formulate a vision for your life of faith? Share some details about that vision.

Support and Challenge

A seasoned Parent in the faith will offer a balanced blend of support and challenge so that growth will occur. Consider four combinations of support and challenge.

High ↑ C H A L L E N G E ↓ **Low**	*Retreat*	*Growth*
	Stall	*Affirmation*

Low ──────── S U P P O R T ─────────→ **High**

Affirmation. *When there is a high level of support but little, if any, challenge to your faith, you merely receive* affirmation for where you are in your journey. The high support will make you feel good about yourself—but you'll go nowhere. High support and low challenge merely preserve the status quo.

 When, if ever, have you experienced this combination of support and challenge? Be specific and then describe its effects on your spiritual growth.

Stall. *When both support and challenge are low,* your spiritual progress will stall. With no mentoring Parent to offer the support and challenge necessary for spiritual growth, you'll feel bad about yourself and go nowhere in your faith. You can too easily become complacent about ever making progress in your spiritual journey.

When, if ever, have you experienced this combination of support and challenge? Be specific and then describe its effects on your spiritual growth.

Retreat. *Too much challenge* without appropriate support can result in retreat, in either burning out or simply dropping out. A Child or Young Adult can lose interest in the spiritual journey and even rebel at some point. Curiously, though, too much challenge may actually cause some Christians to dig in deeper and become tirelessly perfectionistic churchaholics as they seek to measure up to their own expectations, the expectations they assume others have of them, and the probably too-strict expectations they imagine God has.

When, if ever, have you experienced this combination of support and challenge? Be specific and then describe its effects on your spiritual growth.

Growth. *An appropriate mix of support and challenge* results in growth. A balance between support and challenge encourages us to risk entering new territory in our faith, prods us to move on when we get bogged down, and gives us a vision to move toward.

When, if ever, have you experienced this combination of support and challenge? Be specific and describe its effects on your spiritual growth.

 There are occasions on your journey when you will need to ask someone to be a mentoring influence and guide. Whom could you ask? What specifically do you need and/or want from this person? For instance, do you need to advance some skill such as Bible study, witness or prayer, or find personal direction, or overcome some habit that obstructs Christlikeness? And remember, this relationship does not need to be long-term.

Which do you tend to need more from in your relationships—support or challenge? Clarify.

5 Now consider being the believer who offers support and challenge. Suggest at least one way you might perform each of these Parenting functions in your relationships with Children or Young Adults in the faith.

— Providing Support:

— Issuing a Challenge:

— Formulating a Vision:

In your relationships—do you tend to be more like a father who challenges or a mother who supports? Explain. (A mature Parent in the faith will learn to do both!)

Eric Erikson on Midlife

Midlife is a critical time for care-giving and guiding others along the journey of faith, and psychologist Erik Erikson talks about why. (Don't let his big words scare you.) According to his studies in human development, individuals in midlife must confront the issue of "generativity versus stagnation." [4] *Generativity* means establishing, guiding, and passing on the flame to the next generation. It may include rearing children, training students, or serving as a mentor to a younger worker. Generativity refers to all that a person produces and leaves behind as a legacy. In contrast, stagnation results from giving little of one's self to others, from being too involved in themselves and their successes. Stagnation brings with it a feeling of boredom, a life of impoverishment, and an excessive preoccupation with self.

 To whom are you extending Christian support and challenge or to whom could you be offering your guidance and concern? If you're not sure, ask God to show you.

Parenting Do's and Don'ts

Consider the following qualities of effective spiritual Parents:

• Skilled Parents are not overprotective. They do not shield younger believers from pain and the opportunity to learn from life's hard times. • Skilled Parents do not do for others what they can do for themselves. • Skilled Parents do not try to rescue and fix people, and they know that they are not responsible for the happiness of others. • Skilled Parents do not hurry fellow believers through the process of spiritual growth. They understand that each of us has our own unique timetable. • Skilled Parents do not give pat answers, canned advice, or banal formulas for how to lead a Christian life.

Observing and Imitating Parents in the faith

Skilled Parents know that their example can be a catalyst to the growth of a Child or Young Adult. Understanding that we human beings learn by observing and by imitating, skilled Parents know the power of an effective and inspiring model, and therefore the importance of being a model worth imitating. Parents also know that the Child and the Young Adult in the faith need to see Christian values and behaviors not only in a distant hero but especially up close, nearby, and in people with whom they can closely identify. Personal interaction and a strong emotional connection with a Parent in the faith makes that person invaluable on the journey toward spiritual maturity. After all, faith is caught as well as taught. (If you study the following verses, you will be impressed with the value of someone who models a mature Christian faith: Luke 6:40; Philippians 3:17, 4:9; 1 Thessalonians 1:6-7; 1 Timothy 4:12; Hebrews 13:7.)

The Empowering Parent

Just as no two people are alike, no two spiritual journeys are alike. In light of this truth, each of us needs a Parent who understands where we are on our stage of faith and discerns the specific obstacles to our progress. Skillful and loving Parents also calibrate expectations to the particular strengths and weaknesses of each traveler. Furthermore, Parents in the faith are able to empower a Child or Young Adult toward further spiritual growth because they themselves have been working on the milestones of spiritual progress. They can both empower others to reflect and to risk *and* offer a blend of support, challenge, and vision that will help others grow toward Christlikeness.

But whom does God provide to care for and nurtures a Parent in the faith? Our need for support and challenge does not diminish when we become Parents in the faith. The absence of adequate support, challenge, and vision may cause stagnation, resignation, or regression in a Parent just as it can in a Child and Young Adult. Only foolish Parents dare to continue on their journey alone. Wise Parents, therefore, are careful to seek the support of fellow Parents, but they find encouragement, support, challenge, and vision in their relationships with Children and Young Adults in the faith as well.

Before we close this lesson, note the following points.

▶ We are not saying that, prior to middle-age adulthood and the Parenthood stage of faith, you cannot "bear fruit" or serve or disciple fellow believers. Milestone #7 simply emphasizes that ministry grows out of who you are, and Parents in the faith draw from their deep, seasoned Christian life as they guide others.

▶ Christian leaders, pastors, seminary graduates, and missionaries are not automatically in the Parenthood stage. They may be trained and salaried to do what Parents do, but they may not yet be there experientially. As you read earlier, a consistent and coherent Parent stage of faith is unlikely much before the age of forty and then only if the milestones of Childhood and Young Adulthood have been attended to.

▶ Parents in the faith are urgently needed! There is no early retirement for Christians! Children and Young Adults in the faith need a nurturing Parent as they face the complexities of life and the questions that come with living out one's Christian convictions.

Pilgrim in Progress

Complete the following sentence and let it be the first in several sentences that explain your thoughts and feelings.

 The thought of modeling and guiding the growth of other believers makes me think/feel...

Declaring My Priority

Read Philippians 1:21-25 below. When Paul wrote these words, he had been a follower of Jesus for thirty years. Now he was in prison, facing death, reflecting on his life, and re-examining the values he considered ultimate and eternal. With eternity putting the temporal in perspective, Paul affirmed the priority of supporting and challenging fellow Christians along their journey of faith.

> 21 For to me, to live is Christ and to die is gain. 22 But if I am to live on in the flesh, this will mean fruitful labor for me; and I do not know which to choose. 23 But I am hard-pressed from both directions, having the desire to depart and be with Christ, for that is very much better; 24 yet to remain on in the flesh is more necessary for your sake. 25 Convinced of this, I know that I will remain and continue with you all for your progress and joy in the faith.

8 Paul's life purpose was to help other believers make progress and experience joy in their faith. Take some time to seriously reflect on what *you* want to be remembered for. Re-examine the values you consider ultimate and eternal. Is empowering others on their spiritual journey a priority to you? As Paul did, write your thoughts as a prayer of commitment.

Lesson 12

Milestone #8 Seasoned By Time and Experience

The Parenthood Stage:
Modeling Faith

Milestone #7

Empowering Others

To grow spiritually, I need to assume my responsibility to impact other members of God's family, offering experience from my own spiritual journey and guided by the biblical principles of spiritual growth that are reflected in these milestones of faith. I will work to acquire the skills I need to effectively nurture my brothers and sisters toward Christlikeness and wholeness.

Milestone #8

Seasoned by Time and Experience

To grow spiritually, I need to press on, continuing to work on the milestone tasks of spiritual development so that I may know God better. I will not be content to let myself plateau or relax as the years go by. Instead, I will nurture a deepening relationship with my heavenly Father.

In this second milestone of the Parenthood stage of faith, a believer moves into a deep, refined, and stable friendship with God. By this point in the spiritual journey, the veteran Parent knows God and His ways intimately and experientially.

The Parent in the faith has kept the faith over the years—personally as well as publicly. A Parent's faith is now deep and stable, but the passion to know God better and to finish the journey well still burns. So the Parent presses on toward further growth and the strengthening to each of the eight milestones of spiritual development.

Aims of Lesson #12

This lesson offers a new perspective on the relationship between aging and spiritual growth. Plan to spend at least two hours completing this lesson and preparing for your small-group time. During your time of personal study, you will:

◆ Learn about the Apostle John's transformation from the Son of Thunder to the Apostle of Love.

◆ Consider characteristics of mature faith

◆ Look at how issues of aging can impact spiritual growth.

For Small-Group Leaders:

We recommend that during the ninety-minute study portion of this meeting, group members discuss the following questions.

Lesson 12
1-6

You will not be able to give equal time to each question above. So, as group leader, budget your time carefully.

☑ Note:

Before reading through this Milestone, take a moment to glance at your **Spiritual Growth Profile**. Looking briefly at that mirror to your spiritual journey will help you put the coming discussion into the more personal context of your own spiritual growth.

Retracing Our Steps

Since there are no shortcuts to spiritual maturity, middle adulthood (thirty years of age or beyond) is the likely point of entry into the Parenthood stage of faith. The transition happens as a result of tending to the milestones of Childhood and Young Adulthood. In the Parenthood stage, a believer is able to offer to people who are not as far along in their journey of faith a seasoned model worth imitating. Furthermore, the Parent can serve as a skilled guide who knows the spiritual journey from experience, who is able to support and challenge others on their pilgrimage, and who understands how addressing the milestones of Childhood and Young Adulthood helps move a believer toward wholeness and spiritual maturity.

Overview of Milestone #8
Seasoned by Time and Experience

The fathers in the faith whom John addressed are the "spiritually adult in the congregation." [1] They now enjoy a deep, stable, and intimate communion with God, their heavenly Father. In fact, the spiritual fathers to whom John wrote may have known Christ for as many as sixty years. That being the case, the three milestones of the Childhood stage of faith have long been carefully attended to by some in John's audience. Even their struggles to own a firsthand faith, to learn to think Christianly, and to work through the battles of the Young Adulthood stage of faith happened long before John wrote to them. These fathers now possess the depth and stability of mature Christian experience, a depth lacking in the Children and Young Adults in the faith. John Stott writes:

> All Christians, mature and immature, have come to know God. But their knowledge of Him ripens with the years...
> They [the fathers] are already consciously living in eternity... Their first flush of ecstasy in receiving forgiveness and fellowship with the Father was an experience of long ago. Even the battles of the young men are past. The fathers have progressed into a deep communion with God. [2]

Parents in the faith enjoy a rich fellowship with God. Only longtime obedience to His commands and sustained attention to the milestones of spiritual growth—all blessed by the transforming work of the Spirit—can sculpt a mature and fully developed Christlike faith. Maturity comes with the *intensity*, not merely the *extensity* of years.

Each milestone provides opportunities for the believer to experience God in more transforming ways and to become progressively Christlike and whole. These milestones are not ends in themselves. Instead, each is a means to the life-giving friendship with God and a care-giving ministry to others.

Based on 1 John 2:13-14 ("I am writing to you, fathers, because you have known Him who has been from the beginning"), Milestone #8 addresses the core issue of developing and enjoying a rich and mature faith. This milestone calls believers to press on to know God better and to finish their journey well.

Moving Away From... In Milestone #8, you are moving away from stagnation—from the tendency to withdraw or retire; from staying where you are and resting comfortably on the laurels and the results of earlier spiritual growth; from being mentally rigid and closed to new ideas; and from fear and anxiety about aging and physical decline.

Moving Toward... At the same time in Milestone #8, you are moving toward a rich and satisfying faith—toward a deep, proven, stable friendship with God; toward ongoing appraisal and renewal of your spiritual direction and life-giving faith; toward the point where personal holiness and God-given wholeness merge; toward a lifestyle characterized by godly wisdom; toward continuing your long obedience to God and your consistent attention to the milestones of spiritual growth; and toward finishing well your journey of faith.

John's Transformation: From Son of Thunder to the Apostle of Love

Having developed John's "map" of three stages of spiritual growth in this thirteen-week series, now let's briefly consider the story of John's own transformation. When Jesus first invited John to leave his vocation as a rugged fisherman and follow Him, this disciple was nicknamed the Son of Thunder (Mark 3:14): he was loud, self-centered, impetuous, and known for his fiery temperament. Over the next sixty-five years, though, God slowly transformed this high-voltage, impulsive, and ambitious man into the Apostle of Love. We find evidence of John's transformation in the account of Last Supper with His disciples. On the night before Jesus' death, when He was sequestered in the Upper Room with the Twelve, John was seated next to Jesus, the place of honor, having become His closest confidant. John, "the disciple that Jesus loved (John 13:34)," is now content to find his true identity in simply being the object of Jesus' love. He had learned to get close and listen to the heart of God. Church history reports that John, who outlived all the other apostles, became a godly pastor and a faithful elder statesman of the church at the end of the first century. [3] And we can be assured that, as He did with the Son of Thunder, God can transform us as well.

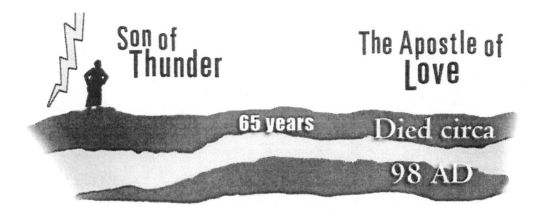

The Goal of Spiritual Growth: Full-Grown Faith

New Testament references to a mature faith (see Ephesians 4:13; Philippians 3:12; and Hebrews 5:14; 6:1) describe that faith as complete, fully developed, fulfilling its potential, and lacking nothing. It's the faith of believers who have lived out their purpose in the Lord and attained the goal or proper end of their existence. [4] This Parenthood in the faith is also the stage where personal holiness and God-given wholeness merge. Only a person whose faith has been seasoned by time as well as by years of walking with the Lord will be blessed with both the divine healing that leads to wholeness and the inner work of the Holy Spirit that leads to holiness.

The need today is for deep people

Richard Foster, noting the cultural factor of immediate gratification that opposes long-term, deep spiritual progress for the Christian, wrote,

> Superficiality is the curse of our age. The doctrine of instant satisfaction is a primary spiritual problem. The desperate need today is not for a greater number of intelligent people, or gifted people, but for *deep people*. [5]

One goal of *Stages of Faith* is to help you understand how to become a deeper, more mature Christian. The journey of faith, the process of maturing in your Christian walk, begins at salvation and ends in a believer's glorification. This growth is a lengthy process: "We are *being transformed*" (2 Corinthians 3:18, emphasis added) from the Childhood stage, to Young Adulthood, and finally to Parenthood in the faith (1 John 2:12-14), always toward a new depth of transformation.

"Knowing Him"

Note the repetition in these two verses: "I am writing to you, fathers, because you know Him who has been from the beginning" (1 John 2:13 and 14) and "I have written to you, fathers, because you know Him who has been from the beginning" (verse 14). E. H. Hiebert, in his commentary on 1 John, notes that John's "assurance concerning their mature knowledge only needed reemphasis. As mature believers they could not afford to relax their spiritual growth." [6]

Recall that John wrote that the "children" (2:13) know the Father (Milestone #2). All Christians have come to know God. But one's knowledge of Him is to deepen with the influence of the years. The elderly apostle John observed that some believers had a personal knowledge of God that had become rich and intimate. Pastor and theologian James Boice writes that

> It is the fathers who, as a result of a lifetime of spiritual experience, have known the Eternal One and have come to fully trust Him... The children are those who have recently come to the knowledge of God and of sins forgiven. The fathers have acquired the gift of spiritual wisdom, having lived longer in the faith and thus have come to know Him who is from the beginning in a deeper way. [7]

Both sufficient time and experience are essential to producing true Parents in the faith. This depth is lacking in believers who are not so far along in the journey.

"Him who has been from the beginning"

We have seen that the "children" have come to know God as their Father. Now, the new, advancing element is the reference to time ("from the beginning"). As we've seen in 1 John 2:13-14, the apostle wrote to people who have known "Him" long and well and described "Him" as the One "who has been from the beginning." But to whom does *Him* refer to—God the Father or Jesus the Son?

The Father's Trustworthiness

In 1 John, the pronoun *Him* seems to refer more often to God the Father, and the word Father does appear twice in the immediate context of 2:15-17. If "Him who has been from the beginning" refers to God the Father, the sentence suggests God's unchanging faithfulness and reliability. Our eternal God does not change as human beings change with advancing years. Our God is forever the same.

Long experience with the Lord brings wisdom as well as deep trust in Him. Christians begin their spiritual growth knowing God as "Father," as their "heavenly Parent" (Milestone #2). They then work to discard any unfounded and distorted ideas they have about God's true character, ideas that delay their spiritual growth. God the Father then re-parents the child. As the years go by and their journey of faith continues, believers may become Parents in the faith, confident that God the Father never changes and is always trustworthy. Time and experience are essential to reaching this level of spiritual maturity.

 The Father is totally reliable and utterly trustworthy. For what current circumstances in your life do you find encouragement in this truth? Explain.

The Son's Pre-existence

In his gospel as well as in his epistles, John taught Jesus' pre-existence and eternal deity. The first verse of 1 John ("What was from *the beginning*, what we have heard, what we have seen with our eyes, what we beheld and our hands handled, concerning the Word of Life" [emphasis added]) and the opening of John's gospel ("In *the beginning* was the Word, and the Word was with God, and the Word was God... And the Word became flesh, and dwelt among us, and we beheld His glory, glory as of the only begotten from the Father, full of grace and truth" (1:1,14 [emphasis added]) support the idea that *Him* refers to Jesus.

When the first-century heretical teachers claimed that the Spirit of the Christ came upon Jesus at His baptism and left Him before His crucifixion and that Jesus was not the unique God-man, the mature Parents in the faith knew better. The Parent in the faith is doctrinally sound and stable, and these fathers whom John addressed would have known the truth about Jesus' identity for many years. They had confronted deception, doctrinal error, and counterfeits to faith before. Again, time plus experience are essential to attaining this level of spiritual maturity.

Seasoned by Suffering

The Parent in the faith is never a stranger to suffering. After all, the Young Adulthood stage of faith, through which a Parent has already journeyed, is an intense time of coming to own one's faith and convictions despite strong opposition from the three arch enemies of spiritual progress. This conflict is the context for coming to know God more deeply. God used John's suffering-- as He uses our suffering-- as part of his transformation. As John MacArthur noted, the apostle John's brother James became the church's first martyr and that each of the other disciples was martyred one by one. "These were John's friends and companions. Soon he alone was left. In some ways, that may have been the most painful suffering of all." [8] Additionally, in his latter years, John was exiled on the harsh island of Patmos, where he lived in a cave, a harsh envoronment for an aged man.

Robert Law, in his commentary on 1 John, observed that a new kind of knowing God results from suffering or conflict. "There is a 'knowing,' that of the children, which must precede the fight; and there is a 'knowing,' that of the fathers, which comes after it." [9] Pain and conflict, fear and doubt, develop the kind of knowing that becomes ours "after the fight."

 Think about a time you experienced conflict or pain. In what way(s) did you come to know God better during that season of your life? OPTIONAL: Or, if you're currently dealing with conflict or pain, why might it prove to be a path toward knowing God better?

 Now read the following verses. What truths are helpful to you as you deal with the pain you are currently experiencing?

Romans 5:3-4   James 1:2-4

Philippians 3:10   1 Peter 5:10

We can be confident that our trials and pain have a definite purpose in God's plan for our life and for our spiritual growth. God uses the hard times to make us tested and seasoned Parents in the faith, and these hard times will become key aspects of the personal testimony that we as Parents in the faith will share with others.

Readiness for the Milestone: Knowing God in Midlife

As we enter adulthood, we confront issues we didn't face when we were younger. These issues can trigger new spiritual growth, and we can come to know God on a deeper level. Research in human development offers clues to understanding the issues that arise with both the progress and the decline that characterize adulthood. Consider how these features of adulthood may trigger the growth of the adult's faith.

Robert Peck, in his research on adult development, notes four challenges that face middle-aged adults:

— With the decline of physical powers, adults must value wisdom rather than physical strength.

— Adults must redefine relationships with both sexes. This includes learning to "socialize" relationships instead of "sexualizing" them. The challenge here is to stress companionship, not sexual intimacy or competitiveness.

— Adults must develop "cathectic" flexibility or face "cathectic" impoverishment. *Cathectic* means "of, relating to, or invested with mental or emotional energy." So Peck is saying that adults need emotional support from soul friends as they face the death of parents and the drifting apart of friends.

— Adults must develop mental flexibility rather than being rigid in their thinking. Often middle-aged adults are stereotyped as dogmatic, set in their ways, and closed to new ideas. Middle-aged adults must be open to fresh ideas and willing to change if they are to continue to grow. [10]

 Apply Peck's ideas to spiritual growth. What message does he have for Christians reaching the Parent stage on their journey of faith?

Bernice Neugarten, in her research on aging, suggested that one of the positive changes that comes at mid-life is "interiority," which she defines as the tendency to be more philosophical and reflective. Middle-aged adults reflect on where they have been in life and where they are going. They also experience a shift in their perspective on time, thinking now in terms of the time left rather than the time since birth. Men in middle age tend to feel increased pressure whereas women tend to find increased freedom and assertiveness as children are soon independent and career opportunities arise. [11]

Daniel Levinson, described the major seasons of adulthood, and advised mid-life adult to take stock of their life. Questions like "Who am I?" and "Where am I going?" become important again at this point of life that is something of a second adolescence. Middle-aged adults evaluate personal achievements in light of their lifelong goals and dreams and begin to set new goals and find a new dream to pursue. [12]

 Now apply the ideas of Neugarten and Levinson to spiritual growth. What message do these researchers have for Christians reaching the Parent stage on their journey of faith?

Readiness for the Milestone: Knowing God *beyond* Midlife

Christians are not immune to the challenges, losses, and struggles that life brings after age forty-five or fifty. Even though life's final chapters are beginning, growth need never stop. Challenges can continue to bring us into a deeper relationship with God. Struggles can further ground us in His truth, His power, and His hope. As we age, we need not decay, plateau, or stagnate spiritually. Knowing God makes the difference.

Erik Erikson identifies the conflict between "integrity versus despair" as the primary issue of older adulthood. Integrity is the emotional integration and sense of coherence and wholeness that enables one to be at peace with oneself in the face of decline and death. In contrast, despair is emotional disintegration, a lack of coherence and wholeness, and the inability to accept one's inevitable death. Despair results in fear and anxiety and the feeling that one's life has not been worth living. [13]

Consider the following list of triggers that can cause either growth (integrity) or stagnation (despair) in adults at mid life and beyond:

Changing cultural values and patterns regarding aging
A sense that your productive life is past
Reaching your life goals
Evaluating your failures and disappointments
Decreasing physical strength
Health challenges
Reduced income
Forced retirement
Leisure time

The ingratitude of those you love
Tragedies
An empty nest
Widowhood
Dependency
The reality and inevitability of death
    take on a new significance

Parents in the faith have been—and continue to be—seasoned by the experiences listed above. Again, knowing God makes a difference as they face the tough issues that come in adulthood. Not surprisingly, success in meeting these challenges depends, to a great extent, on how well believers have mastered the skills of the milestones of Childhood and Young Adulthood.

 Choose three or four items from the list of triggers above and explain why knowing God can help the believer face those events.

A Review of the Parenthood Stage of Faith

We've asked the questions "What does the spiritual maturity look like?" and "Where is this lifelong journey of faith taking me?" and found some answers to those questions in Milestones #7 and #8. [If you have completed the "Spiritual Growth Profile," refer to the results of the five items for each of the two Milestones.]

Milestone #7—Empowering Others

As a mature believer, I intentionally enter into care-giving relationships with others in order to empower them on their spiritual journey. I resist simplistic formulas and prescriptions in guiding others toward wholeness and Christlikeness. I offer a compelling witness to the deep spiritual reality I have experienced, drawing on my own unique story of God's work in my life.

If I were to neglect this milestone, I would slow the progress and healing of other believers whose spiritual growth requires a relationship with experienced and skilled guides. If I do not sufficiently develop the essential skills of nurturing others and mediating grace to believers confronting the truths of each of the milestones, their spiritual health and growth may be impoverished.

Milestone #8— Seasoned by Time and Experience

Decades of time and life-experience are required to forge a deep and mature believer. As a veteran of the faith, I have come to know God and His ways intimately and experientially, and I know Him to be utterly reliable. My passion is to finish the journey of faith well and for His glory alone.

If I were to neglect this milestone, my spiritual growth would plateau, and I would fall short of the depth of Christlike character and transformation God desires for His children.

Mature Parents in the faith have travelled far on the journey. Their progress is seen when we recall the apostle John's three evidences of genuine faith: obedience, love, and discernment.

The Evidence of Obedience. John emphasized the vertical dimension of faith, the evidence of Obedience, in 1 John 2:3-6; 2:28-3:10; and 5:2-3. Mature faith and love for God have been developed over the years by both time and experience. The Parent now richly abides in Christ, knows God deeply, and practices His Word. The Parent now walks much as Jesus walks, and the resemblance is compelling.

The Evidence of Love. John addressed the horizontal dimension of faith, the evidence of Love, in 1 John 2:7-11; 3:11-18; 4:7-21; and 5:1-3. When believers are in the Parent stage, their love for others is manifested in its most mature expressions. Now experienced in care-giving and in guiding others toward spiritual maturity and wholeness, the believer extends God's love and healing grace to others, and that love empowers them towards spiritual transformation and Christlikeness. The Parent now loves much as Jesus loves, and the resemblance is striking.

The Evidence of Discernment. John highlighted the evidence of Discernment in 2:18-27; 4:1-6; and 5:1,4,5. The Parent has come to identify counterfeits to authentic faith, counterfeits in their own spiritual growth as well as in other believers. And, of course, this discernment involves far more than noting doctrinal deficiencies of cults and ably defending orthodox faith. This wise believer discerns the lies that detain other believers' progress at the Child, Young Adult, and Parent stages of faith. The Parent now sees much as God sees, and the resemblance is convincing.

A Pilgrim's Satisfaction

Besides incarnating God's character and being deeply rooted in the obedience, love, and discernment, Parents in the faith live with the keen awareness that only a life focused on and grounded in the eternal is fully meaningful. Parents clearly understand that they are on a pilgrimage to another country (Hebrews 11:14; 13:14), and this understanding gives purpose and meaning to their everyday life. For the Parent in the faith, eternity is now concrete, as real as anything ever touched!

Consider what C.S. Lewis wrote about this pilgrimage:

> Creatures are not born with desires unless satisfaction for those desires exists. A baby feels hunger: well, there is such a thing as food. A duckling wants to swim: well, there is such a thing as water. Men feel sexual desire: well, there is such a thing as sex. If I find in myself a desire which no experience in this world can satisfy, the most probable explanation is that I was made for another world. If none of my earthly pleasures satisfy it, that does not prove that the universe is a fraud. Probably earthly pleasures were never meant to satisfy it, but only to arouse it, to suggest the real thing. If that is so, I must take care, on the one hand, never to despise, or be unthankful for these earthly blessings, and on the other hand, never to mistake them for the something else of which they are only a copy, or echo, or mirage. I must keep alive in myself the desire for my true country, which I shall not find till after death; I must never let it get snowed under or turned aside; *I must make it the main object of life to press on to that other country and to help others to do the same* [emphasis added]. [14]

Malcolm Muggeridge and C.S. Lewis warn us to not become earthbound and instead grow to the point where we desire something that no earthly pleasure can satisfy.

> "The only ultimate disaster that can befall us,
> I have come to realize, is to feel ourselves
> to be at home here on earth.
> As long as we are aliens,
> we cannot forget our true homeland." (Muggeridge)

> "Our Father refreshes us on the journey with some pleasant inns,
> but will not encourage us to mistake them for home." (C.S. Lewis)

A Closing Prayer

Almighty and loving God, thank You that You have called me to travel this pilgrimage to You... and thank You that I do not travel it alone.... Forgive me for the doubts and mistrust that come at bumps in the road... and please help me to endure when the journey gets difficult.... Thank You that You are a redeeming God who uses our pain for a good purpose. I believe that truth, God—help my unbelief.... And, Lord, I want to know You better. Make me thirsty and then satisfy that thirst with Yourself... and with Your love so that I may love others.... Use me to encourage fellow believers, to empower them on their journey, and to share my personal story of Your love, Your healing, and Your faithfulness. Keep me ever grounded and growing in You. I pray in Jesus' precious name and for His sake. Amen.

Lesson 13

Celebrating Your Progress

By now you are well acquainted with the stages of faith, you know about the milestones to be attended to along the journey of spiritual growth, and you have shared much about yourself with your group. It is also quite likely that you have made some significant progress toward spiritual maturity and wholeness in Christ. This lesson will help you bring closure to your study of spiritual growth.

For Small-Group Leaders:

We recommend that during the ninety-minute study portion of this meeting, group members discuss the following questions.

Lesson 13
1, 3-4

You will not be able to give equal time to each question above. So, as group leader, budget your time carefully.

The Traveler

Spiritual growth is not merely the accumulation of knowledge. Genuine learning about God is transformative. Truly learning about God means getting to know Him better, and that knowledge changes us. Mature Christians move past knowing facts about God to experiencing His presence with them in an intimate and constant way. That kind of communion results in healing, wholeness, and Christlikeness. Hear this point made three other ways:

> "Education with inert ideas [i.e., isolated facts] is not only useless: it is, above all things, harmful.... It must never be forgotten that education is not a process of packing articles in a trunk."

> "To act as though learning is a matter of stacking facts on top of one another makes as much sense as thinking one can learn a language by memorizing a dictionary."

> Educator Charles Gragg dismisses "the assumption that it is possible by a simple process of telling to pass on knowledge in useful form. This is the greatest delusion of the ages. If the learning process is to be effective, something must happen in the learner."

At one level of this study, you have learned about a biblical, multidimensional model of spiritual growth. At another level, you will have—**by God's grace**—gained some skill in living out these truths and applying other insights you have gained.

After all, this study was designed to help you:

- ◆ Understand a biblical model of spiritual growth
- ◆ Determine where you are on your spiritual journey
- ◆ Identify what work you need to do on each milestone
- ◆ Discover what may be blocking God's healing touch and impairing your spiritual progress
- ◆ Experience God's restorative grace for your hurts, habits and hungerings
- ◆ Learn how to mentor and guide believers of all ages and at all stages on their journey of faith

1 ✎ Evaluate what you've learned as you've studied *Stages of Faith*. Toward which of the goals listed above are you making some progress? In which area(s) of your life have you experienced/are you experiencing a degree of transformation? (It's often difficult to see our own growth. Someone who knows you well may need to help you answer this second question.)

The Route

The biblical model of spiritual growth that we've looked at is based on 1 John 2:12-14. The apostle's map can help you see how far you've traveled, the distance remaining on your journey, and possible routes you can take to your destination. However, as Gary Jennings points out below, maps lie.

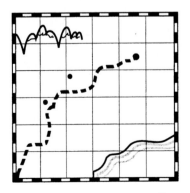

Even the best of maps... are liars, and they cannot help being liars. That is because everything shown on a map appears measurable by the same standards, and that is a delusion. For instance, suppose your journey must take you over a mountain. The map can warn you of that mountain before you get to it, and even indicate more or less how high and wide and long it is, but the map cannot tell you what will be the conditions of terrain and weather when you get there—or what condition you will be in. A mountain that can be easily scaled on a good day in high summer by a young man in prime health may be a mountain considerably more forbidding in the cold and gales of winter, to a man enfeebled by age or illness and wearied by all the country he has already traversed. Because the limited representations of a map are thus deceptive, it may take a journeyer longer to travel the last fingerbreadth of distance across a map than it took him to travel all the many handspans previous. [1]

2 What does this warning say to you about the 1 John 2:12-14 map for your spiritual journey?

A Letter from Your Heavenly Father

3 As you've studied 1 John and various other passages of Scripture, you've been reading from a letter your heavenly Father wrote to you long ago. Now it's time for you to write to yourself an even more personal letter from Him. On a separate sheet of paper, write the letter that you think God would write to you as you close this book. What key truth(s) does God want you to take away from your study of the stages of faith? What does He want you to be sure to remember? What would He say to encourage you at this point of your journey?

When you've finished, put the letter in your Bible so that it can remind you of how far you've come and where you're going on your journey of faith. At the final meeting, you may want to share your letter with the group.

Encouraging Words for Your Fellow Travelers

4 At your next and final meeting, be ready to tell your fellow travelers on this journey one specific thing that you have come to appreciate about each of them. You might also choose to comment on growth you've noticed in their life. Feel free to be creative as you prepare for this time of encouragement and celebration of all that you have shared. You might, for instance, write your thoughts on cards and give them to the group members. You might even give a flower or another small symbol of growth to each group member.

A Closing Prayer

Have someone in the group read aloud the verses from Psalm 84 printed below. Let those words set the tone for a time of group prayer, a time of lifting before the Lord the areas of both progress and struggle your fellow travelers have shared, and a time of thanking God for calling you to take this journey and for enabling you to do so.

Psalm 84:5,7

Blessed are those whose strength is in You,
who have set their hearts on pilgrimage.
They go from strength to strength,
til each appears before God in Zion.

Happy are they who, nerved by thee,
set out on pilgrimage!
They are the stronger as they go,
til God at last reveals himself in Zion.
(Moffatt Translation) 2

Tips for the Small-Group Leader

Inviting People to Your Stages of Faith Study

When you invite people to your *Stages of Faith* group, give them a clear sense of the purpose and plans of the group that you're asking them to join. Make the words your own so that the invitation is heartfelt and sincere, but here's one idea to get you started: "I'm excited about starting a small-group study on an interesting book I've read. It's called *Stages of Faith*, and I think you'll find it different from anything else around. We'll be meeting together to do three things: to share (build friendships), to study *(Stages of Faith)*, and to support one another (prayer and encouragement). I'd really like you to join us."

If the person seems interested, share a little more information: *"Stages of Faith* gives us a map of spiritual growth and helps us look closely at how we are growing spiritually. Each of us will figure out where we are on this biblical map. You can expect to spend about ninety two hours each week getting ready for the meeting. So this group does involve a commitment—but it's definitely worthwhile. I'm sure you'll find it challenging and renewing. You don't have to decide right away. Think about it and pray about it, but I hope you'll join us."

Share the following information about what's ahead so that no one will be surprised:

- ◆ We'll meet thirteen times, we'll do one lesson each meeting, and I'll be leading.
- ◆ We'll meet on (day of week) for two hours from_____to_____.
- ◆ The first meeting will begin on (date)_____and the last one on (date)_____.
- ◆ We'll meet at (address):_____. (Supply a map if needed.)
- ◆ An introductory meeting—we call it a "Huddle"— will give us the opportunity to get to know one another. I'll hand out the *Stages of Faith* book and introduce the study. (See pages 116-117, "How-To's for a Successful *Stage of Faith* Group.")
  Huddle date:_____.

- ◆ Share the names of people who will be in the group.

- ◆ Emphasize that completing the lessons will enhance their learning experience as well as the quality of the group's discussion.

- ◆ Explain that you'll call them on a specific date to ask for a decision and that you'll be praying for in the meantime—and then be sure to pray!

- ◆ Encourage people to invite a friend. If he or she is interested, talk with that person. "If they are interested, let me know, and I'll follow up."

- ◆ Finally, be sure to ask, "Do you have any questions?"

How-To's for a Successful Stages of Faith Group

Begin with a Huddle:

One week before the first meeting, get together to do the following:

- Pass out the *Stages of Faith* books and Spiritual Growth Profile. (Get book and Spiritual Growth Profile to anyone who doesn't come.)
- Assign group members to complete the first lesson in *Stages of Faith* for your first meeting. It will take about two hours of preparation.
- Assign group members to complete the Spiritual Growth Profile by the second lesson. It takes about twenty minutes to answer the forty questions and another fifteen to finish the graphs. As the group leader, you will want to complete the Spiritual Growth Profile before the Huddle so you can be ready to offer any help.
- Share your enthusiasm about the group and the journey toward a more mature faith that you are embarking on together.
- Plan a creative way to get group members better acquainted. After you introduce yourself, have people introduce themselves and have them share something relatively nonthreatening about themselves (what they like to do in their free time, what was their favorite vacation and why, why they came to the study, etc.).
- The "Group Guidelines" (below) will help the group members clarify expectations. Plan on spending thirty minutes on this.
- Close with prayer for one another as you begin this journey.

Group Guidelines

At your Huddle, clarify your expectations for the group meetings and finalize details about of the *Stages of Faith* study. A handout is an easy way to do this. Note the four questions to discuss in your Huddle.

- **Dates:** We will meet together on (day) _____ for thirteen weeks.
Our beginning date is _____. Our projected ending date is _____.

- **Time:** Each session will begin at_____ and end promptly at _____.

- **Attendance:** Please make these meetings a top priority and be there unless an emergency arises. If you need to be late or absent, please let me know beforehand. *To share:* Do I see any obstacles to my timely arrival and regular attendance?

- **Preparation:** Plan to spend approximately two hours on the lesson before you come to the meeting.
To share: Where will I carve out the time to study and prepare?

- **Participation:** I encourage each of you to participate in the sharing, study, and support aspects of this group. Building friendships, working through *Stages of Faith*, encouraging one another, praying for one another—keeping these things in balance will make for a rich and rewarding session for all of us. I also ask that you be sensitive to the limited amount of time we have. All of us need to be sure to give everyone in the group an opportunity to talk. *To share:* Why is participation important to becoming a good, strong group?

- **Confidentiality:** What's shared in the group, stays in the group! Let's agree to not gossip or repeat what another group member has said, and help make this group a safe place.

- **Openness:** In a good group, we will to try to be a window and not a wall. As well as we are able, let's reveal who we are, and where we are in our spiritual growth—faults and all. Let's be honest with God, the questions in the *Stages of Faith* text and with each other. *To share:* What may happen to a group if members do not bring openness?

- **Sensitivity:** Let's attempt to put ourselves in one another's shoes and understand what it is like to be you, and really listen to what you have to say. Let's not try to 'fix' or advise each other.

- **Leadership:** Each of us can play our own part in making this a successful and purposeful group, and we do this as we do our do our best to keep us focused on our goals.

- **Prayer:** Of course, we will pray for the other group members, and know they are praying for each of us.

Budget Your Time

Ask group members to work through the lesson and answer every question in preparation for the meeting. At the meeting, however, you may not have time to discuss every question, so choose those questions that are, from your prayerful perspective, most valuable to the group members. The author of this Stages book has recommended questions to discuss at the beginning of each lesson.

We recommend that you complete *Stages of Faith* in thirteen meetings. Only then will group members gain a panoramic view of the process of spiritual growth. If a few lessons are particularly important to your group and the sharing is deep and personal, let the sharing continue rather than cutting it short in order to complete a lesson. Don't do that too often, though. That's not fair to folks who have prepared their lesson and need or want to talk about a question you haven't yet addressed. Also, be sure you have the whole group's support if you sense some members want to meet for longer than the agreed-upon number of weeks.

The Leader's Roles

The small-group leader is a facilitator, not a lecturer. The leader's job is to enable the group to accomplish its goals of sharing, study, and support. The group members themselves are responsible for working toward those goals.

Each two-hour meeting will include the following three elements.

#1. Sharing:

In order to build deeper friendships, your group will learn how to listen to and care for one another as the weeks go on. The questions you answered in *Stages of Faith* at home invite self-disclosure and building community. The few minutes for refreshments and mingling at the beginning of the meeting also helps build friendship.

#2. Study:

In order to cultivate personal growth, your group will learn what God's Word says and then work together on applying its truths to your lives. You will always hold one another accountable to move beyond *knowing to doing*. Each of the thirteen lessons focuses on a single element of one of the stages of spiritual growth. The questions are designed to help you learn about yourself and your walk of faith. You'll spend a bulk of our meeting time (ninety minutes) studying. According to those who have done this study before you, great is the reward when you take time outside of the group to prepare each lesson.

After the sharing question you—as the group leader—will present a brief overview for the lesson by referring to "Retracing Our Steps" and "Moving Away From... Moving Toward..."

Remind group members to answer every question in the text as they work through the lesson in preparation for the meeting. At the meeting, however, the group will not have time to discuss every question from the lesson. That's why certain questions for discussion are suggested at the beginning of each chapter. They can serve as an outline for your "Study" time, and of course you may choose your own questions. After all, you know the members of your group.

The following ideas may help you to lead the group toward a rich "Study" time.

1. The group leader can personally ask a group member to come to the next meeting prepared to share one of the questions of the lesson, and their answer, that seemed to cause the most thought or response in them. Give them a time limit. That is likely to pave the way for others to share at a personal and deep level.

2. As the leader of the group, you will want to occasionally lead as in #1 above. This will model for the group the kind of sharing you would hope for.

#3. Support:

Lessons may bring up feelings, memories, hurts, and issues that group members have neglected. Rather than deny these injuries, your group can risk talking about them and giving themselves permission to feel the pain and in this setting where they will also find care and prayer support. Finally, you'll close your group with ten or fifteen minutes of encouragement and prayer.

Evaluating Our Group

1. From Time to Time

From time to time, ask an experienced group member to pay special attention to the leadership, communication, and overall group dynamics so that he/she can offer feedback to the group at the end of the meeting.

Leadership was	Dominated by one person	Dominated by a sub group	Centered in about half the group	Shared by all members of the group
Communication was	Badly blocked	Difficult	Fairly open	Very open and free-flowing
People were	Phony	Hidden	Fairly open	Honest and authentic
The group was	Avoiding its task	Loafing	Getting some work done	Working hard at its task

2. The Group's Six-Week Checkup

At the end of the sixth meeting, ask group members complete the "Six-Week Checkup" (pages 132-133). Take ten minutes of the seventh meeting to discuss any relevant findings and begin to make necessary adjustments according to the participants' input.

1. Rate the group's effectiveness in achieving its three goals. Circle a number from 1 to 10, with "1" being a poor performance and "10" an excellent performance.

  a. Sharing: 1 2 3 4 5 6 7 8 9 10

  b. Study: 1 2 3 4 5 6 7 8 9 1

  c. Support: 1 2 3 4 5 6 7 8 9 10

What might we do to better achieve those goals we are not yet reaching effectively? Be as specific as possible.

2. Which of the following diagrams best illustrates our group's communication?
  L = leader; D = dominant group members.

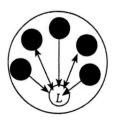 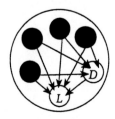 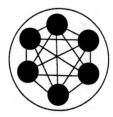

3. Rate how easily the group is side-tracked by certain individuals or interrupted by circumstances. Let "1" be "We're more off track than on" and "10" be "We never wander."

1   2   3   4   5   6   7   8   9   10

What might we do to get back on track when we digress?

3. Guidelines

Evaluate your performance in the group. How are you doing when it comes to meeting the following standards that you and the other group members agreed to initially? Again, "1" is a poor performance and "10" an excellent performance.

a. Time: I get to the meeting on time so that the group can begin when it is supposed to.
1   2   3   4   5   6   7   8   9   10

b. Attendance: I give priority to group meetings and attend unless there is an emergency.
1   2   3   4   5   6   7   8   9   10

c. Preparation: I complete my lessons before the meeting.
1   2   3   4   5   6   7   8   9   10

d. Participation: I share, but I don't let myself dominate the time. I actively listen when others speak.
1   2   3   4   5   6   7   8   9   10

e. Confidentiality: I keep everything that is shared confidential.
1   2   3   4   5   6   7   8   9   10

4. Communication Assessment

Put a dot on the line somewhere between ALWAYS and NEVER in response to each of these statements about your small group.

	ALWAYS	NEVER
We respect one anothers' opinions.	_____	
We make an effort to listen well.	_____	
We are not afraid of emotions.	_____	
We seek to affirm one another wherever we are on our spiritual journey.	_____	
We refrain from giving advice.	_____	

The FAQs about Stages of Faith

• *Do the stages of faith you discuss refer to chronological ages or metaphorical stages?*

These stages were outlined by the apostle John. so we must ask the question of him: Was he taking note of chronological ages or identifying levels of spiritual maturity? According to theologian John Stott, "[John the apostle] is indicating not their physical age, as some have thought, but stages in their spiritual development, for God's family, like every human family, has members of different maturity ... They represent three different stages of spiritual pilgrimage." [1] F.F. Bruce observed, "The threefold grouping relates to spiritual maturity not years reached by the calendar." [2] But, as you will see, age is a critical factor in our spiritual growth. Time and experience definitely help us move toward maturity.

• *How many groups of people was John addressing?*

The clearest and least confusing interpretation of the biblical text is that the author divided his readers into three groups, and he addressed each group twice.

Group One	Group Two	Group Three
Little children (teknia)	Young men	Fathers
Children (paidia)	Young men	Fathers
1 John 2:12, 13	1 John 2:13, 14	1 John 2:13, 14

Repetition of these designations as well as of the messages addressed to them (messages which are similar if not identical) is no doubt intended for emphasis.

• *In what ways is teknia ("little children" in verse 12) different from paidia ("children" in verse 13c)?*

The term teknia, translated "little children," is used only by John. An expression of affection and endearment used in the context of family, this term emphasizes the community that will foster Christian growth. Throughout his epistle, John emphasized this interdependent life together.

The term paidia, which means "children," refers to the infant, the baby, the very young child who is dependent and in need of training, guidance, protection, and nurturance. Paidia is found twice in 1 John, in 2:13c as we've seen and in 2:18. That second reference introduces a passage on living in the "last hour." Apparently in verses 18-27 John was addressing Christians in the Childhood stage of faith who are still particularly vulnerable to deception.

• *Why did John speak to the children, the fathers, and, last, the young men?*

Why doesn't the order follow a consecutive, chronological sequence? One theory is that, by placing them last, John emphasized "young men" in the faith, that critical stage where many adults plateau and stall. This theory would also explain why John described the stage of Young Adulthood more fully than he did the other two stages. Another possibility is that John gave the two extremes first (the beginning and the end) and then the intermediate stage, "young men." Finally, throughout the epistle of John, we find sharp contrasts between light and darkness, love and hate, truth and error. Here, possibly, is the contrast between child and parent, with the reference to young men following.

• *Why did John change verb tenses from "I am writing" to "I have written"?*

John began his first three statements with "I am writing you" (present tense) and the second three with "I have written you" (aorist tense). Some commentators suggest that "I have written you" refers either to a former letter (and the present-tense verbs to 1 John) or to the earlier part of the epistle (and the present verbs to the letter as a whole). The aorist is probably an aorist tense suitable for letters in which case there is really no difference in meaning between the aorist tense and the present tense. In fact, the New International Version translates all six occurrences as the present tense "I write to you."

One more note on biblical scholarship in this study. Great care has been taken to allow the biblical text to speak for itself. Only after establishing the meaning of the biblical passage do we turn to research in human development for clarification about some of the growth patterns and clues about the dynamic process of faith growth throughout life. The exegetical evidence from 1 John 2:12-14 (some of which you have just reviewed) is a strong foundation for the model of stages of spiritual growth presented in this text. Know, too, that Stages of Faith combines the *content* of faith and the *process* of faith.

The Eight Milestones of Spiritual Development

The faith stages of Childhood, Young Adulthood, and Parenthood are each marked by distinct milestones. Those milestones, derived from and therefore consistent with the biblical teaching, are focal points in the Stages of Faith lessons.

The Childhood Stage of Faith

Milestone #1 Experiencing God's Grace and Forgiveness
"Your sins are forgiven you for His name's sake." (2:12)
Milestone #2 Embracing God as Father
"I write to you, children (paidia)
because you have known the Father" (2:13c)
Milestone #3 Growing Up Together
"little children" (teknia, 2:12)
The relational context in which growth will occur.

The Young Adulthood Stage of Faith

Milestone #4 Owning a Firsthand Faith
"You are strong" (2:14)
Milestone #5 Linking Truth and Life
"The word of God abides in you" (2:14)
Milestone #6 Defeating the Enemies of Spiritual Growth
"You have overcome the evil one" (2:13, 14)

The Parenthood Stage of Faith

Milestone #7 Empowering Others
"fathers" (2:13, 14)
Milestone #8 Seasoned by Time and Experience
"You know Him who has been from the beginning" (2:13, 14)

Other Biblical Support for the Stages of Faith Model

First John 2:12-14 is not the only biblical passage that describes the process of spiritual growth. Many other Bible texts help us understand the journey of faith (see below). Nor is 1 John 2:12-14 a complete theology of spiritual formation. However, no other biblical writer identified as clearly as John did three separate stages of spiritual development and the distinguishing characteristics of each stage. Below are other biblical clues about the process of spiritual growth (my emphasis is added).

• *Every Christian is commanded to pursue and experience spiritual growth. Note the variety of ways this truth is expressed:*
"Do not be conformed to the world, but *be transformed.*" — Romans 12:2
"You received from us instruction as to how you ought to walk and please the Lord, that you may *excel still more.*" —1 Thessalonians 4:1
"Let us *press on to maturity*" —Hebrews 6:1
"Long for the pure milk of the word, that by it you may *grow in respect to salvation.*" —1 Peter 2:2
"*Grow* in the grace and knowledge of our Lord and Savior Jesus Christ." —2 Peter 3:18

• *The ultimate goal of our faith journey is Christlikeness. This end will become the centering hope of each Christian who makes the pilgrimage.*
"Whom He foreknew He also predestined to become conformed to the image of His Son." —Romans 8:29
"We all... are being transformed into the same image from glory to glory." —2 Corinthians 3:18
"[You] have put on the new self who is being renewed... according to the image of the One who created him." —Colossians 3:10
"When He appears we shall be like Him... And everyone who has this hope fixed on Him purifies himself, just as He is pure." —1 John 3:2-3

• *The process of spiritual growth should continue through one's life.*
"We are no longer to be children... We are to *grow up...* to a mature man." —Ephesians 4:11-16
"Not that I have already obtained it, or have already become perfect [mature], but *I press on.*" —Philippians 3:12
"So that you may walk in a manner worthy of the Lord... *increasing* in the knowledge of God." —Colossians 1:10

• *Individuals have traveled different distances on their journey toward maturity. The process of growth and change is both predictable and sequential, though not irreversible or guaranteed.*
Some believers are "weak" and others are "strong" —Romans 14-15
Some are carnal "babes," stuck in infancy (1 Corinthians 3:1-3), while others are "spiritual" (2:15).
Paul wrote that there was a time when he was a "child" and later a "man" when he did away with childish things —1 Corinthians 13:11.
According to Philippians 1:25, some believers needed Paul's care-giving to insure their "joy and progress in the faith." This verse highlights emotional and spiritual growth as well as the value of having a guide for the journey of faith.
Some believers are "dull of hearing... a babe," and others are "mature" —Hebrews 5:11-14.
Some have "suffered shipwreck in regard to their faith" —1 Timothy 1:19

The unique contribution of 1 John 2:12-14 is to clarifies that this growth toward spiritual maturity takes place in three predictable stages. These verses suggest eight milestones that, attended to, will catalyze growth or, left undone or incomplete, will impede progress.

• *What is the role or place of spiritual disciplines in the journey of faith?*
Prayer, reflection, solitude, silence, fasting, worship, and simplicity are all means of opening one's self to God, and that openness to God's transformational work in us is key to John's model. This model, however, suggests that a Christian may practice these disciplines wholeheartedly and regularly, yet remain frozen in the Childhood stage of faith. Also consider, too, that these practices will be experienced in very different ways by the believer in the Childhood, Young Adulthood, and Parenthood stage of faith. The practice of these disciplines is simply not a reliable measure of either the distance or the depth of one's journey of faith. First John 2:12-14 is like a map identifying the landmark issues of our journey, and the classic spiritual disciplines can definitely enrich the traveler along the way if the believer is able to focus on the disciplines as a means to an end, not as ends in themselves.

The Spiritual Growth Profile

 Medical doctors relies on sophisticated technology to diagnose or repair physical health and growth. The educator looks to standardized tests to predict classroom success. The coach eyes the athlete's skills and potential with stop watch and statistics. How can we to measure the Christian's spiritual growth and progress? Adults are eager to know how far and deep they are along the journey of faith. The Spiritual Growth Profile can help you understand your spiritual health and progress, locating where you are on the journey toward full grown maturity and Christlikeness. Then, you can begin to chart steps to take that can lead to renewal and growth.

Some instruments that purport to measure spiritual growth focus on quantifiable and external behaviors, such as disciplines of Bible study, memorization, and witness, etc. Such instruments simply do not describe a picture of how far the believer has traveled on the journey of faith. They do not see the believer in process, nor report the condition of the believer's inner world. Too, such instruments do not offer adequate explanations of what obstacles might delay their spiritual growth. There are other instruments, such as the Spiritual Well-Being Scale, Intrinsic-Extrinsic Religiosity, Spiritual Maturity Index, and Religious Status Inventory, which are of limited value or interest to the Christian believer who desires to see where they are spiritually in a biblical framework. Know that in his research, the author has carefully taken steps to determine and insure the validity and reliability of the Spiritual Growth Profile.

The *Spiritual Growth Profile* Is Different

The Spiritual Growth Profile is designed to highlight a Christian's strengths and deficiencies in the stages of Childhood, Young Adulthood, and Parenthood of the faith. The Spiritual Growth Profile consists of forty items to which the respondent indicates his "likeness" using a Likert Scale of 1 to 7. You receive clear instructions on how to score your own Journey of Faith Chart which will graphically show the respondent's progress at each of the eight Milestones. An informative four page Manual will help you interpret your Journey Chart and your SGP scores. I know of no other instrument like this.

A Biblical "Map"

The Spiritual Growth Profile and Journey Chart show where the respondent locates himself on the 1 John 2:12-14 "map" of the journey of faith. The items will help you determine: How far you have traveled, Where you are strong, What may be delaying your growth and progress and, Where you can go deeper and farther as a Christian. Once you have before you your own Journey of Faith Chart, you can attend to any obstacles which delay your spiritual growth. The *Stages Of Faith* text will help clarify the milestones you need most to work on. Each lesson focuses on gaining understanding and skills needed for each stage.

For Individuals, Faith-Shapers and Small Group Leaders

All individuals will benefit from locating their progress, as well as faith-shapers, and small group leaders. A small group could begin the *Stages of Faith* study with each group member completing and scoring their own the SGP. The group leader can remind the group members to check their Chart as they work on lessons in the book. If you are a faith-shaper, knowledge of the Journey Chart of those in your care will enable you to develop tailor-made strategies of spiritual direction. Too, counselors, teachers, Christian educators, church leaders, and pastors will gain insight as to how we grow spiritually, why this growth plateaus or stagnates, and what they can do to nurture others toward full grown spiritual maturity.

To order the *Spiritual Growth Profile* packet, contact:

Don Willett, Ph.D.
408 N. Broadway Suite E
Redondo Beach, CA 90277

(310) 374-5953; FAX (310) 374-3511
don.willett@adelphia.net
Cost is only $10.00 each.

Endnotes/Recommended Resources

Preface

1. Stott, John. *The Epistles of John*. Grand Rapids, Michigan: Eerdmans Publishing Co., 1991. page 101.

Childhood In the Faith
Lesson One

1. Stott, John. *The Epistles of John*. Grand Rapids, Michigan: Eerdmans Publishing Co., 1991. page 101.

Lesson Two... Task #1, Part 1

1. Sloat, Donald. *Growing Up Holy and Wholly* . Brentwood, Tenn.: Wolgemuth and Hyatt, 1990. p. 196.
2. Packer, J. I.. *Knowing God*. Downers Grove, Illinois: InterVarsity, 1973, p. 41.

Recommended Resources for Milestone #1:
1. Certainty of Salvation:
Bright, Bill. *How to be Sure You Are a Christian*. Campus Crusade for Christ, 1981.
Srombeck, J. F. *Shall Never Perish*. Eugene: Harvest House, 1982.
Swindoll, Charles. *Eternal Security*. Portland: Multnomah Press, 1981

2. Identity Formation:
Briggs, Dorothy. *Your Child's Self-Esteem*. New York: Doubleday and Co., 1975.
McGee, Robert. *The Search for Significance*. Rapha, 1990.
Narramore, Bruce. *You're Someone Special*. Grand Rapids: Zondervan, 1978.
Wagner, Maurice. *Put It All Together*. Grand Rapids: Zondervan, 1974.

Wagner, Maurice. *The Sensation of Being Somebody*. Grand Rapids: Zondervan, 1975.

Lesson Three... Milestone #1, Part 2

Recommended Resources for Milestone #2:
Elkin, Frederick & Handel, Gerald. *The Child and Society. The Process of Socialization*. Fifth Edition. NY: Random House, 1989.
Henslin, Earl. *Forgiven and Free*. Nashville: Nelson, 1991.
Jabay, Earl. *The God Players*. Grand Rapids: Zondervan, 1969.
Narramore, Bruce, and Counts, Bill. *Guilt and Freedom*. Irvine: Harvest House, 1974.
Seamands, David. *Healing of Damaged Emotions*. Wheaton: Victor Books, 1981.
Seamands, David. *Healing Grace*. Wheaton: Victor Books, 1988.
Smedes, Lewis. *Shame and Grace. Healing the Shame We Don't Deserve*. San Fransisco: Zondervan Publishing House, 1993.
Stoop, David. *Hope for the Perfectionist*. Nashville: Thomas Nelson, 1987.
Swindoll, Charles. *The Grace Awakening*. Dallas: Word, 1990.
Thurman, Chris. *The Lies We Believe*. Nashville: Thomas Nelson, 1989. See Chapters 2: "Self-Lies"; and chapter 6, "Religious Lies".

Lesson Four... Milestone #2

1. Tozer, A.W. *Knowledge of the Holy*. New York: Harper and Row, 1961, p. 10.
2. Nouwen, Henri. *The Return of the Prodigal Son*. New York: Doubleday, 1992.
3. Gaultiere, William and Christi. *Mistaken Identity*. Old Tappan, NJ: Revell, 1989. p. 21.
4. Seamands, David. *Healing of Damaged Emotions*. Wheaton: Victor Books, 1981. pp. 55-72. See Chapter, *"Creating God in Your Parents' Image."*
5. ibid. *Healing of Memories*. Wheaton, Illinois: Victor, 1985. See Chapter 7, *"Distorted Concepts of God."* pp. 107-120.
6. Ten Boom, Corrie. *In My Father's House*. p. 58.
7. Seamands, David. *Healing of Memories*. Wheaton, Illinois: Victor, 1985. pp. 100-101.
8. Phillips, J.B. *Your God Is Too Small*. New York: Macmillan, 1961.
9. Johnson, David and Van Vonderen, Jeff. *The Subtle Power of Spiritual Abuse*. Minn: Bethany House Pub., 1991. p. 42.

Recommended Resources for Milestone #2:

Hyde, Kenneth. *Religion in Childhood and Adolescence*. Birmingham: Religious Education Press, 1990. See Chapter 3: "Children's Ideas of God"; Chapter 4: "Parental Images and the Idea of God."

McClung, Floyd. *The Father Heart of God*. Eugene, Oregon: Harvest House, 1985.

Narramore, Bruce. *No Condemnation*. Grand Rapids: Zondervan Press, 1984.

Nouwen, Henri. *The Return of the Prodigal Son*. New York: Doubleday, 1992.

Packer, J. I.. *Knowing God*. Downers Grove, Illinois: InterVarsity, 1973. See Chapter 19: "The Sons of God".

Phillips, J. B. *Your God Is Too Small*. New York: Macmillan, 1961.

Stoop, David. *Making Peace with Your Father*. Wheaton, Illinois: Tyndale, 1992.

Additional verses on God as Father: Psalm 68:5-6; Psalm 103:8-13; Isaiah 30:18; Matthew 6:9; 7:7-11; John 16:27; 2 Cor. 1:3; 6:18; Ephesians 1:1-14; 3:14-19; Hebrews 1:5b.

Lesson 5, Milestone #3, Part I

1. Stott, John. *One People*. Downers Grove: Illinois, InterVarsity Press. p. 78.

Lesson 6, Milestone #3, Part II

1. Goldberg, Herb. *The New Male*. New York: William Morrow and Company, 1979, p. 17

Recommended Resources for Milestone #3:

Backus, William. *Untwisting Twisted Relationships*. Minneapolis: Bethany House, 1988.

Crabb, Larry. *Encouragement*. Grand Rapids: Zondervan, 1984. See Chapter 9, "Truth and Relationships".

Crabb, Larry *Inside Out*. Grand Rapids: Zondervan, 1990.

Greenfield, Guy. *We Need Each Other*. Grand Rapids: Baker, 1984.

Johnson, David and Frank. *Joining Together: Group Theory and Group Skills* (Fourth Edition). Englewood Cliffs, New Jersey: Simon and Schuster, 1991.

Powell, John. *Why Am I Afraid to Tell You Who I Am*. Niles, Ill.: Argus Communications, 1969.

Powell, John. *Why Am I Afraid to Love*. Niles, Illinois: Argus Communications, 1972.

Richards, Lawrence. *A Theology of Christian Education*. Grand Rapids: Zondervan, 1975.

Smith, David. *Men Without Friends*. Nashville: Thomas Nelson, 1990.

Welch, Reuben. *We Really Do need Each Other*. Nashville, Tennessee: Benson Publishing Co., 1973.

Young Adulthood in the Faith
Lesson 7, Milestone #4

1. Arndt and Gingrich, *A Greek-English Lexicon of the New Testament*. Chicago: University of Chicago Press, 1957, p. 384

2. Shelton, Charles. *Adolescent Spirituality*. Chicago: Loyola University Press, 1983. p. 72.

3. Fowler, James. *Stages of Faith*. San Fransisco: Harper and Row, 1981, p.

4. Shelton. *Adolescent Spirituality*. p. 72.

5. Johnson, Alan. *Romans, Volume II, The Freedom Letter*. Chicago: Moody Press, 1985, p. 119.

6. Dunn, James. *Romans 9-16*. Word Biblical Commentary, Vol. 38. Dallas: Word Books, 1988, p. 795.

7. Cranfield, C.E. *The Epistle to the Romans*. The International Critical Commentary, Vol. 2. Edinburgh: T. & T. Clark Limited, 1979, p. 812.

8. Stifler, James. *The Epistle to the Romans*. Chicago: Moody Press, 1960, p. 223.

9. Nygren, Anders. *Commentary on Romans*, Philadelphia: Fortress Press, 1949, p. 445.

10. Westerhoff, John. *Will Our Children Have Faith?* New York: The Seabury Press, 1976. See Four Styles of Faith in Chapter 2.

Lesson 8... Milestone #4, Part II

1. Stonehouse, Catherine. *Patterns in Moral Development*. Waco: Word, 1980. Adopted from p. 36.

2. Fowler, James. *Stages of Faith*. San Fransisco: Harper and Row, 1981, pp. 151-173.

3. ibid. *Stages of Faith*. San Fransisco: Harper and Row, 1981, pp. 174-183.

Recommended Resources for Moral and Faith Development/Milestone #4:

Hyde, Kenneth. *Religion in Childhood and Adolescence*. Birmingham: Religious Education Press, 1990.

Joy, Donald. *Moral Development Foundations*. Nashville: Abingdon Press, 1983.

Kohlberg, Lawrence. *The Philosophy of Moral Development*. Vol. I. New York: Harper and Row, 1981.

Sell, Charles. *Transitions. The Stages of Adult Life*. Chicago: Moody Press, 1985. See Chapters 8-9.

Shelton, Charles. *Adolescent Spirituality*. Chicago: Loyola University Press, 1983. See Chapter 3-4 on spirituality and the adolescents' developmental experience.

Stokes, Kenneth. *Faith is a Verb*. Mystic, Conn: Twenty-Third Publications, 1989. See Chapter One: "The Concept of Faithing"; Chapter Two: "The Journey of Faith". Includes Westerhoff's Styles of Faith and Fowler's Stages of Faith.

Lesson 9... Milestone #5

1. Shelton, Charles. *Adolescent Spirituality*. Chicago: Loyola University Press, 1983. pp. 33-42.

2. Bee, Helen. *The Journey of Adulthood (Third ed.)*. Prentice-Hall Co., 1996. pp. 150-183.

3. Packer, J. I.. *Knowing God*. Downers Grove, Illinois: InterVarsity, 1973, p. 50.

4. Richards, Larry. *Creative Bible Study*. Chicago: Moody Press, 1970, p. 75.

5. Habermas, Richard and Issler, Klaus. *Teaching for Reconciliation*. Grand Rapids: Baker Book House, 1992, pp. 104-107.

Recommended Resources for Milestone #5:

Munger, Robert Boyd. *My Heart Christ's Home*. Downers Grove, IL.: InterVarsity Press, 1986.

Raths, Lois; Harmin, Merrill; Simon, Sidney. *Values and Teaching*. Columbus, Ohio: Merrill Pub. Co., 1978.

Sheldon, Charles. *In His Steps*. Grand Rapids: Zondervan, 1967.

Steele, Les. *On the Way, A Practical Theology of Christian Formation*. Grand Rapids: Baker Books, 1990. See Chapter 12, "Cycles of Christian Formation in Adults".

Lesson 10... Milestone #6

1. Stott, John. *The Epistles of John*. Grand Rapids, Michigan: Eerdmans Publishing Co., 1991. page 102.

Recommended Resources for Milestone #6:

Anderson, Neil. *The Bondage Breaker*. Eugene, Oregon: Harvest House Publishers, 1990.

Bubeck, Mark. *The Adversary*. The Christian versus Demon Activity. Chicago: Moody Press, 1975.

Bubeck, Mark. *Overcoming the Adversary*. Chicago: Moody Press, 1984.

Elkin, Frederick and Handel, Gerald. Fifth Edition. *The Child and Society. The Process of Socialization*. New York: Random House, 1989.

Stott, John. *The Epistles of John*. Grand Rapids, Michigan: Eerdmans Publishing Co., 1991.

Wiersbe, Warren. *The Strategy of Satan: How to Detect and Defeat Him*. Wheaton, Illinois: Tyndale House, 1979.

PARENTHOOD in the Faith
Lesson 11... Milestone #7

1. Vine, J. (1989). *Exploring 1,2,3 John*. Neptune, NJ: Loizeaux Brothers. p. 31.

2. Robert Mulholland. *Invitation to a Journey. A Road Map for Spiritual Formation*. Downers Grove: InterVarsity Press, 1993. p. 15.

3. Daloz, Laurent. *Mentor. Guiding the Journey of Adult Learners*. San Fransisco: Jossey-Bass Publishers, 1999. pp. 203-229.

4. Bee, Helen. *The Journey of Adulthood*. New York: Macmillan Publishing Co. 1987. p. 62.

Recommended Resources for Milestone #7

Berry, Carmer Renee. *When Helping You is Hurting Me; Escaping the Messiah Trap.*

Clinton, Bobby. *Please Mentor Me.* 1991.

Coleman, Robert. *Master Plan of Evangelism.* Old Tappan, NJ: Flemming Revell Co. 1964.

Daloz, Laurent. *Mentor. Guiding the Journey of Adult Learners.* San Fransisco: Jossey-Bass Publishers, 1999. See Chapter 8, "The Yoda Factor: Guiding Adults through Difficult Transitions", pp. 209-235.

Erikson, Eric. *Identity and the Life Cycle.* W. W. Norton and Company, Inc. 1980.

Hagberg, Janet. *The Critical Journey.* Salem, WI: Sheffield Publishing Company. 1989.

MacDonald, Gordan. "Disciple Abuse". *Disciple Journal.* Volume 5, no 6, Issue 30 (Nov. 1, 1985).

Richards, Lawrence. *A Theology of Christian Education.* Grand Rapids: Zondervan, 1975. See Chapter 8, "A Modeling Method."

Steele, Les. *On the Way: A Practical Theology of Christian Formation.* Grand Rapids: Baker. 1990. See Chapter 12, "Cycles of Christian Formation in Adulthood."

Lesson 12... Milestone #8

1. Stott, John. *The Epistles of John.* Grand Rapids, Michigan: Eerdmans Publishing Co., 1991. page 102.

2. ibid. *The Epistles of John.* Grand Rapids, Michigan: Eerdmans Publishing Co., 1991. page 102.

3. MacArthur, John. *Twelve Ordinary Men.* The W Publishing Group. Nashville: Tenn., 2002. page 100.

4. Arndt and Gingrich, *A Greek-English Lexicon of the New Testament.* Chicago: University of Chicago Press, 1957, pp. 816-817.

5. Foster, Richard, *Celebration of discipline: The path to spiritual growth.* New York: Harper and Row, 1978. page 1.

6. Hiebert, E. H. (1988). An Expositional Study of I John. *Bibliotheca Sacra.* 145, 420-435.

7. Boice, James Montgomery. *The Epistles of John.* Grand Rapids: Zondervan. 1979. p. 72, 74.

8. MacArthur, John. *Twelve Ordinary Men.* The W Publishing Group. Nashville: Tenn., 2002. pages 113-114.

9. Law, Robert. *The Tests of Life.* Third edition. Grand Rapids: Baker. 1914. p. 313.

10. Peck , Robert. "*Psychological Development in the Second Half of Life*", in *Middle Age and Aging.* ed. Bernice Neugarten. Chicago: The University of Chicago Press, 1968, pp. 82-92.

11. Neugarten, Bernice. *Middle Age and Aging* , ed. "The Awareness of Middle Age". Chicago: The University of Chicago Press, 1968, pp. 93-98.

12. Levinson, Daniel. *Seasons of a Man's Life.* New York: Ballantine Books. 1978.

13. Erikson, Eric. *Identity and the Life Cycle.* W. W. Norton and Company, Inc., 1980, pp. 103-105.

14. Lewis, C.S. *Mere Christianity.* New York: Macmillan Publishing Company, 1943, p. 120.

Recommended Resources for Milestone #8:

Alexander, Donald (Editor). *Christian Spirituality: Five Views of Sanctification.* Downers Grove, Illinois: InterVarsity. 1988.

Bee, Helen. *The Journey of Adulthood.* New York: Macmillan Publishing Co. 1987. See Chapter 10, "Spiritual Development and the Search for Meaning".

Erikson, Eric. *Identity and the Life Cycle.* W. W. Norton and Company, Inc. 1980.

Foster, Richard. *Celebration of Discipline; The Path to Spiritual Growth.* New York: Harper and Row. 1978.

Gormly, Anne and Brodzinsky, David. *Lifespan Human Development.* New York: Holt, Rinehart and Winston, Inc. 1989. See Chapters 13-17, on middle and later adult development. Neugarten, Bernice. Middle Age and Aging. Chicago: University of Chicago Press. 1968. Senn, Frank (Editor). Protestant Spiritual Traditions. Mahwah, NJ: Paulist Press. 1986.

Willard, Dallas. *Spirit of the Disciplines.* San Fransisco: Harper and Row. 1988.

Lesson 13

1. Jennings, Gary *The Journeyer.* p.170.

2. Moffatt, James. *The Bible.* New York: Harper and Row, 1922.

Answers to Commonly Asked Questions

1. Bruce, F.F. *The Epistle of John.* Old Tappan, New Jersey: Fleming Revell Co, 1970. p. 59.

2. Stott, John. *The Epistles of John.* Grand Rapids: William B. Eerdmans Publishing Co, 1991. p. 96.